On Alert!

ON ALERT!

ON ALERT!

Staying Vigilant through Prayer

by
Rob Fischer

SUMMIT
Leadership Series *for* Men

On Alert!

Copyright ©2014 Rob Fischer

All rights reserved.

ISBN-13: 978-1495316470

ACKNOWLEDGEMENTS

I appreciate Pastor Nathan Rector for writing the Foreword for this book and the whole *Summit Leadership Series for Men*. Ray Edwards and Perry Underwood, two of my "comrades in arms" helped me tremendously in the formation of this series through their creative ideas and prayers. I'm also grateful to my daughter Heather for her creative cover design and to Jan Mitchell for her keen eye proofing the manuscript. My loving wife, Linda, has been a source of joy and encouragement to me in all our pursuits for nearly 40 years. Finally, I dedicate this book and series to my Lord and Savior, Jesus Christ.

TABLE OF CONTENTS

Foreword ii

Introduction 1

Chapter 1 – **Following Skills** 17

Chapter 2 – **Call to Action** 31

Chapter 3 – **What Is Prayer** 49

Chapter 4 – **How to Pray** 69

Chapter 5 – **Praying Conversationally with Others** 93

Appendix – **Additional Resources** 121

Other Books by Rob Fischer 123

About the Author 125

FOREWORD

Rob Fischer's heart for men's discipleship is evident to all who know him. I am grateful that in *Summit – Leadership Series for Men* he has poured out that heart into an engaging, challenging, and life-changing resource. Whether you are looking to grow in your own faith or are looking for a resource to assist you in leading others, this book is a must read!

Nathan Rector,
Senior Pastor,
Valley Real Life, Spokane Valley, WA

INTRODUCTION

In December 2001, I moved to Anchorage, Alaska. I've always been an avid hiker and I could hardly wait to explore as much of Alaska's "last frontier" as possible. The fact that I arrived in December shouldn't put a damper on my quest, right?

The Chugach Mountain range presents a formidable boundary blocking Anchorage's sprawl to the east. Among those peaks closest to Anchorage is Flattop Mountain. Flattop owns the distinction of being the most-climbed mountain in Alaska. But I'd venture to guess that 99.9 percent of those climbs occur in the few summer months of the tourist season. During the winter, however, the mountain gets a cold, lengthy retreat from the onslaught of hikers.

Don't be fooled by Flattop's popularity as a hiking destination. People die on its slopes from time to time either due to falls or avalanche. Twice I helped rescue climbers who were hurt or unable to come down the mountain on their own. Often the weather conditions—exaggerated on the mountain—have forced me to abandon plans of summiting.

But when I first arrived in Alaska, I was a novice and didn't know what I didn't know. So, on a beautiful sunny, but cold January day I set out to hike up Flattop's 1500-foot-elevation-gain. The official summer trail lay under feet of snow, so I merely followed the tracks of the few others that had snow-hiked on the mountain.

The contour of the hike up Flattop divides into four stages: an easy uphill hike around Blueberry Hill; a traverse around the slope and steep climb to the saddle; switchbacks through a rock slide to an upper saddle; and then a very steep scramble (hands and feet) up solid rock to the summit.

On that January day, I had easily reached the backside of Blueberry Hill and had started the traverse around the mountain where I thought the summer trail must lead. What I didn't realize was that I was on the lee side of the mountain, meaning that all the snow had been dumped on this side. Owning to its very steep slope with little to hold the snow in place, I was treading on avalanche-prone territory!

In addition to that, the snow was so hard-packed by the wind that kick-stepping with my heavy boots only gained me perhaps an inch purchase on this extremely steep slope. Unfortunately, I had worked my way around the mountain far enough that I was at the point of no return.

Standing nearly upright against the snow-covered slope with my toes clinging to tiny foot-holds, I looked around to assess my situation. Below me the mountain dropped away several hundred feet. I had no way to self-arrest if I started to slide or fall. I didn't feel comfortable returning the way I'd come, knowing that I'd already pressed my luck getting to where I was.

Continuing to traverse around the mountain only would've gotten me into deeper trouble. Due to my inexperience, I had no idea how stable the snow face was that I was clinging to. So, I decided I would have the most control by climbing up over the crown of this slope and then work my way back down where it was less steep.

I breathed a prayer to God for safety and forgiveness for placing myself in such a dangerous position. I made it up that slope and then off the mountain without mishap, but I was shaken to the core. I knew how close I had come to serious injury or death.

As I continued down the easier trail around Blueberry Hill and back to the trailhead, I reluctantly resigned myself to staying out of these wild mountains in the winter.

A couple winters had passed since that incident, but I still looked longingly at the snow covered Chugach Mountains wishing I could be out there climbing them. I expressed my longing to a friend one day and he told me matter-of-factly, "Greg G. climbs Flattop all winter long."

A day or two later, I happened to run into Greg. "Greg, I understand you climb Flattop all winter long. Would you take me up sometime, show me the ropes, and teach me to hike safely in the winter?" To my surprise, Greg fired back, "How about Thursday?" Truth be told, after my scare on the mountain, I suddenly felt like I needed more time to psych myself up, but I accepted his invitation before I could change my mind.

That Thursday, we met at the trailhead at about 3 pm. I vividly remember Greg telling me that the temperature was minus nine degrees Fahrenheit as he handed me an ice-axe and we began our ascent. We hiked slowly and deliberately as Greg tutored me on winter hiking in the mountains. We stopped along the way and he demonstrated how to arrest a fall using the ice axe and then he had me try. He pointed out trouble spots and areas known to be avalanche-prone.

We were on the switchbacks above the first saddle when the sun set. We were kick-stepping up this steep, snowy slope. Greg had instructed me to walk in his steps. Greg kept training me and imparting everything he could think of to keep me safe and enable me to enjoy hiking in these Alaska mountains in the winter.

Soon, we were kick-stepping up the extremely steep final stage of the climb. The bare rock in the summer becomes engulfed in snow in the winter, but renders the snow stable due to its grip within the deep furrows of the rock. Nevertheless, the steep slope and the fact that this is the leeward side of the mountain combine to form a cornice at the summit. What this means is that the final ascent is near vertical.

As I was kick-stepping and plunging my ice axe into the snow up the final ascent, I was so scared I could feel my muscles tensed and shaking. This gave me a flashback to the close call I had experienced a couple years before on this mountain. I was also anxious about the climb back down, since climbing down is usually more difficult than climbing up. Greg continued to coach me up and through my fear.

We reached the summit, high-fived each other and I laughed nervously. I felt more like the mountain had conquered me, than I had conquered it. We found ourselves in twilight by now and we turned and looked down on the lights of Anchorage. What a beautiful sight! And we were the only two guys enjoying it from this vantage point. But my enjoyment of the view was short-lived. I knew we now had to climb down and I was scared to death! The impending darkness wasn't helping matters.

Then Greg announced, "We're going to use some different techniques to climb down." Then he walked over near the edge of the cornice and said, "Come over here and watch what I do. Give me time to get down a ways and situated and then I'll call to you to follow me so you can come down the way I did." With that Greg turned toward this steep snow chute and simply stepped off! He continued taking long-strides—or *plunge-stepping*—about fifty feet down the chute.

Greg showed me that the snow was up over his knees and softer than where we had climbed up. But knowing the terrain underneath the snow, it was still quite stable. As steep as this chute is, he explained that with the ice axe and the self-arrest techniques he had taught me, I would be safe.

So, following Greg's example I stepped off the mountain plunge-stepping down to where he was. It was exhilarating! From there we sat down in the snow and glissaded (a fancy term for sliding on your butt) about 500 feet down the chute in seconds. We used our ice axes as a brake so we wouldn't lose control. In order to work back to the trail, we traversed to the saddle and continued down the mountain on the safer windward side.

Greg's coaching and training opened up a whole new world of winter hiking for me that I enjoy immensely to this day.

Men, if it's not apparent already, let me say it outright, "I'm a hiking nut!" Through hiking I find solitude, great exercise, opportunity to worship the Lord through the beauty of His creation, partnership with other men who also enjoy hiking, and to borrow a phrase from Eric Liddel, "I feel God's pleasure when I hike![1]

In addition to all that, I often use hiking as a metaphor for life. A couple of my spiritual partners, Perry

Underwood and Ray Edwards have encouraged me to capitalize on the hiking metaphor for this series, *Summit – Leadership Skills for Men*.

Well, after my initial hike with Greg up Flattop Mountain in the winter, I followed him up Flattop two to three times a week all that winter. Since then, I've led many other men up that mountain showing them what Greg showed me. But I had to be really good at *following* before I could *lead*.

In our walk with Christ, many of us attempt to *lead* others without ever having learned to *follow* Jesus. The analogy breaks down here from the standpoint that we will never come to the point in which we no longer need to follow Jesus. As Christ-followers, *we must always lead others by following Christ*.

Few of us will ever lead millions as Joshua did. But before Joshua was ready to lead the nation of Israel, he learned how to follow Moses. In fact, until Moses handed the "baton" to Joshua, Joshua was known as his "young aid" and his "assistant." Moses also taught Joshua how to follow the Lord, so that it was said of Joshua, "he followed the Lord wholeheartedly." (Numbers 32:12)

The Apostle Paul, one of the greatest leaders the church has ever known said, "Follow my example, as I follow the example of Christ." Jesus says to us today as He said to others back then, "Follow Me." If you want to *lead*, you've got to become really good at *following* Jesus Christ.

Perhaps you're thinking, "I would never climb a mountain in the winter *and* I don't want to lead others." Forget about the mountain climbing! It's not everybody's passion. But God *has* called you to lead. A leader is essentially an *influencer* of others. In every walk of life: as a husband, father, grandfather, employer, employee, etc., we men are called upon to influence others for the cause of Christ. You *are* a leader. But to lead others well, we must follow Jesus well.

A friend of mine frequently reminds me, "The way *up* is *down*." What he means by that is what Jesus also explained in Luke 9:23, "Whoever wants to be my disciple must deny themselves and take up their cross daily and follow me." John the Baptist put it like this; he said of Jesus, "He must increase, but I must decrease." (John 3:30 ESV) Our ascent to the heights of relationship with Christ requires humility. We must become skilled at following Him.

The apostle Paul, now an old man, experienced adventurer, and sufferer for Christ's sake, was writing as a prisoner from Rome. With clarity of mind that comes from knowing he was near death, Paul strips away nonessentials and reveals *his ultimate goal* in life. This is *the summit* that trumps all other summits!

> *Yes, everything else is worthless when compared with the infinite value of knowing Christ Jesus my Lord. For his sake I have discarded everything else, counting it all as garbage, so that I could gain Christ and become one with him. I*

> *no longer count on my own righteousness through obeying the law; rather, I become righteous through faith in Christ. For God's way of making us right with himself depends on faith. I want to know Christ and experience the mighty power that raised him from the dead. I want to suffer with him, sharing in his death, so that one way or another I will experience the resurrection from the dead! (Philippians 3:8-11 NLT)*

Paul reveals here that nothing else, no other goal, no other "summit" comes close to that of knowing Christ. *Knowing Christ is our ultimate goal, our daily press to the summit.*

This men's leadership series provides a set of tools to work with that I'm calling *following skills*. Similar to the tools and techniques of winter alpine hiking, these following skills are not an end in themselves, but a means to an end. The following skills enable us to "ascend the summit" of knowing Christ more profoundly. The result of our relationship with Him is a transformed life!

There's one other crucial element to these following skills that parallels back country hiking in Alaska. When hiking in the Alaskan back country, we observe a cardinal rule: *never hike alone!* I know seasoned hikers and adventurers who paid a serious price when they ignored that rule. The same principle applies to our walk with Christ.

Have you ever considered the fact that when Jesus called His disciples to follow Him, He didn't merely call them to *Himself* but *to each other* as well? Jesus calls you and me into a *fellowship of brothers*. We are *Comrades in Arms*.[2] Just as I learned the skills of winter alpine hiking from Greg, we learn to follow Jesus primarily *from others* who are following Him well. "Follow my example, as I follow the example of Christ." (1 Corinthians 11:1)

Many men balk at the idea of *needing* other men to help them in their walk with Christ. Get over it! God created us for relationship with Him *and* others. No one ever does anything of significance alone! There's always a partner or a team. We men have a warped sense that by teaming up with others in our walk with Christ we are somehow "cheating," or diminishing our manhood. Nothing could be further from the truth!

No one leads in a vacuum—that is without followers. And no one can truly follow Christ in a vacuum—without others. We need each other, help each other, and learn from each other. For this reason, I challenge you not to read this book or engage in this series alone. Find at least one other man of kindred spirit and work through this series together.

So what are the *following skills?* I don't know of an exhaustive list of *following skills*. In the Appendix I've listed several sources for additional reading on the subject.[3] For purposes of this book and the others in this series let's discuss and experiment with these *following skills:*

- Reading, study & application of God's Word
- Personal & Corporate Prayer
- Worship
- Solitude
- Service
- Rest
- Fasting
- Spiritual Partnership

I've repeated this Introduction and the first chapter in each book of this series. The reason for this repetition is twofold: first, the information in this introduction is foundational to this whole series. Second, the books in this series are not sequential and each stands on its own.

Finally, I'll be sticking with a hiking metaphor throughout this series. Each book and chapter are peppered with stories from my alpine experiences. Along these lines, consider what a hiker Jesus was during His ministry on earth. He hiked all over Israel on foot, logging hundreds of miles.

Using Google Maps, we find that the walking route from Nazareth to Jerusalem is 150 km! Jesus *walked* that route and farther several times a year just to attend the various annual festivals in Jerusalem. Frequently, He would climb a mountain to get away and pray (Luke 5:16 & 6:12).

You may not be a hiker, but I hope you'll enjoy my story-telling and the close connections I'll draw between hiking and following Jesus.

I look forward to our hike through this series together. But I must warn you, I hike at a brisk pace!

Your brother in Christ,

Rob Fischer

Introduction Discussion Questions

1. Think of a time when you inadvertently put yourself in a dangerous position. What happened? What did you learn from your experience?

2. Why is it necessary to become good at following Jesus in order to become good at leading others?

3. What does it mean to *follow* Jesus Christ today? Unpack Luke 9:23, "Whoever wants to be my disciple must deny themselves and take up their cross daily and follow me."

4. Rob mentioned that the following skills are not an end in themselves but a means to an end. Why is this distinction important?

5. Describe our ultimate goal or summit as followers of Christ.

6. Discuss the idea that following Christ is not a solo pursuit, but that we need to pursue Christ in the company of other men.

7. What is the purpose of the following skills and why is it vital that we keep that purpose before us?

8. What is your experience with the following skills up to now? Which ones do you rely on most heavily? Which ones would you like to explore and experiment with more? In what ways have the following skills posed a challenge to you in the past?

9. In what key way is God speaking to you through this chapter? What will you do about it?

10. Pray with and for each other. We will go over the guidelines of praying with others in chapter 5, but for now simply follow these practices as you pray with each other:

- Pray *short*, phrase or sentence prayers (Don't hog the conversation!)
- Listen to the Holy Spirit and each other
- Piggyback on each other's prayers. Stay on a theme until it seems right to move on
- Keep your prayers vertical (God-ward)
- Embrace silence as an opportunity to listen to God, transition to another topic, or process what has been prayed
- Believe the best of each other

---

[1] Eric Liddel was a Scottish Olympian who won the gold medal in 1924 in the 400m race. He devoted the rest of his life to serving the Lord in China as a missionary.

[2] Rob Fischer, *Comrades in Arms—The Power of Pursuing Christ in the Company of Other Men*, (Spokane Valley, WA: Fischer Publishing, 2013).

[3] I am employing the term "following skills" in place of the traditional term "spiritual disciplines" for purposes of this series. For additional resources on these following skills or spiritual disciplines, please see Appendix.

.

— Chapter 1 —

FOLLOWING SKILLS

He guides me along the right paths for his name's sake.
Psalm 23:3

Through a unique opportunity that I initiated, I had received feedback from a half-dozen friends and family who knew me well. They all agreed. I had a problem losing my cool in traffic. At times, my behavior included outbursts of anger and other un-Christlike responses. This was no new revelation to me and in the past whenever I had a blowup, I had always been smitten immediately in conscience and confessed it to the Lord. But as of yet, I had done nothing to *end* this destructive pattern.

Like I said, when I received the anonymous feedback from those close to me, their assessment came as no surprise. And I thought, "Well, they all do know me well (chuckle, chuckle)." And I was going to leave it at that. Then, in one of those holy moments, God's Spirit spoke to me firmly yet lovingly, "No, Rob, I want to change this about you. As one of My children, this behavior is inappropriate."

I was immediately humbled and realized that although I had known about this pattern of sin in my life and found it offensive, I had been content to deal with it *reactively* whenever it reared its ugly head. Now God was asking me to *proactively* root it out of my life—but how?

How do we change? How do we rid ourselves of patterns of sin? How do we eradicate ungodly thoughts and behaviors that have become a part of us over many years? What is *God's role* in the process of our spiritual transformation and what is *our role?* Let me share with you *five pivotal principles* that address these questions.

The first pivotal principle we've already touched on. We saw in the Introduction that Paul expressed that no other goal, no other "summit" comes close to that of knowing Christ. *Knowing Christ is our ultimate goal, our daily press to the summit.*

Many men start out with a significant, life-changing introduction to Jesus Christ and step into relationship with Him. But unfortunately, many don't move ahead from there. We may often reflect back on our initial introduction to Christ when we came to know Him, but our relationship with Him has stagnated or not progressed since then.

We do well to remember how we came to Christ. But if the extent of our relationship with Christ dwells in the past, then we remain spiritual infants (1 Corinthians 3:1; Hebrews 5:13). We do better to actively pursue our *relationship* with Christ daily, striving to grow into spiritual manhood (Ephesians 4:14-16).

For many Christian men, this principle is not as obvious as it seems. Many of us have assumed that *becoming more like Christ* should be our chief goal, our summit. But think about it, if becoming more Christlike were *the ultimate goal*, then knowing Christ better merely becomes the *means* to reaching that goal!

Whoa! Deepening our relationship with Christ is not merely the *means* to some end. Knowing Christ *is* the ultimate goal, our summit! Remember, "Everything else is worthless when compared with the infinite value of knowing Christ Jesus my Lord."

Knowing Christ and pursuing an ever-deepening relationship with Him is and always will be our chief aim. This is the first pivotal principle.

The second pivotal principle flows from the first: *our spiritual transformation results from knowing Christ, not vice-versa*. We can easily fall into the trap of thinking that we must change ourselves in order to draw closer to Christ. But this is impossible! Only by drawing close to

Christ are we changed. This is the primary thesis of Paul's letter to the Galatians.

A number of years ago, my wife and I bought a 40-year-old home in Spokane, WA, with beautiful mature maple and spruce trees in the yard. Truth be told, we bought the home more for our love of the yard and trees than the house itself. However, only days after moving in, Spokane was hit with an ice storm that downed trees, limbs and power lines. The most majestic of our maple trees lost 16 enormous limbs. We were deeply saddened. There was nothing to do but saw them up for fire wood.

Our relationship with Jesus Christ is much like that maple tree and its branches. Unless the branches remain on the tree, they will die and dry up. Instead of the maple tree, Jesus spoke of our relationship with Him using the metaphor of a grape vine. He said, "I am the vine; you are the branches. Whoever abides in me and I in him, he it is that bears much fruit, for apart from me you can do nothing." (John 15:5 ESV)

This vine and branches metaphor leaves no question about the necessity of relationship. The branch simply must remain on the vine or it will die. The person who abides in, lives in, dwells with, remains in, stays attached to Jesus not only lives, but thrives, *bearing fruit*. Apart from an abiding, ever-growing relationship in Him, not only is there no fruit—there is no life!

Again, this second pivotal principle states: *our spiritual transformation results from knowing Christ, not vice-versa*.

The third pivotal principle is especially relevant to us as we consider the *following skills*. *The purpose of the following skills is to help us know Christ better.* We often make a huge mistake in this regard.

In the movie, *Hitch*, Will Smith plays the role of a "date doctor" by the name of Alex "Hitch" Hitchens. While coaching other men how to attract and win over women whom they secretly love, Hitch finds himself wanting to pursue the beautiful Sara Melas (played by Eva Mendes). Hitch is arrogantly confident of and intensely focused on his *skills* and *techniques* as a dating professional.

So when Hitch orchestrates an elaborate date with Sara, he expects positive results. Instead, she sees through his schemes and wants nothing to do with him. It's not until Hitch abandons his dating *system* and focuses instead on *loving* Sara that she responds in kind.

In a similar way, we men often view the following skills such as reading the Bible and prayer as the best combination with which to *win* Christ's favor. We become preoccupied with *our* skills, techniques, and activity instead of with our Lord and King. Many actually replace deep relationship with Christ with their own self-discipline. But it's not the *following skills* that change us, Christ does!

Following skills like studying the Bible or prayer serve as tools to assist us in deepening our relationship with Christ. Following skills don't transform us, Christ does. The following skills are only helpful and meaningful as they lead us into deeper relationship with Christ. Again, *the purpose of the following skills is to launch us into deeper relationship with Christ.*

The fourth pivotal principle explains that *evidence of spiritual maturity is Christlikeness (or godliness), not how much or how well we practice the following skills.*

I was a senior in high school and captain of the gymnastics team. Our coach sent us home over the two-week Christmas break with individual training assignments. The training regimen and goal he gave me was to come back in two weeks able to perform 25 pull ups and 25 handstand pushups consecutively. Six days out of seven for the next two weeks I trained and pushed myself until I was able to meet my coach's expectations.

I had fun disciplining myself to be able to accomplish those feats. I also found great pleasure in knowing that my ability to knock off 25 of each exercise impressed others. However, I had to admit that my ability to execute those exercises *did not prove my ability as a gymnast.* Instead, those exercises were merely *methods* for helping me become a better gymnast. Our real goal was for each of us on the team to execute our gymnastic routines with perfection so we could win our gymnastic competitions.

The *following skills* are much like those pull ups and handstand pushups. I could not gauge my ability as a gymnast by how many pull ups I could do. Being an accomplished gymnast involves far more than strength. Doing pull ups was simply a means to a greater end.

Similarly, although our ability to perform a following skill may be fun and rewarding, *we cannot determine our spiritual maturity based on our ability to execute a following skill*. The following skill is merely a means for knowing Christ better. And as a result of our relationship with Christ, He transforms us, making us more like Him.

This fourth pivotal principle reminds us that the *evidence of spiritual maturity is Christlikeness (or godliness), not how much or how well we practice the following skills*.

The fifth pivotal principle states that *spiritual transformation requires both dependence and diligence*. Let's consider the dependence side of the equation first. As we've already discussed, spiritual transformation comes about through our relationship with Christ. We are a branch on the vine.

This branch-on-the-vine metaphor demonstrates that *we are totally and utterly dependent on Christ* for producing "fruit" or godliness in our lives. Jesus said, "For without me, you can do nothing." The Apostle Paul expressed the same concept in different terms when he stated, "I have been crucified with Christ and I no longer live, but Christ lives in me. The life I now live in the body, I live by faith in the Son of God, who loved me and gave himself for me." (Galatians 2:20)

This life-transforming work is *God's work* in our lives. The Holy Spirit changes us. This spiritual transformation the Bible also calls *sanctification*. Sanctification is the process of becoming more like Christ in our character. Our sanctification is a lifelong process and something that *we are totally dependent on Christ* to perform in us.

Just like salvation, *our sanctification* (the process of becoming godly or Christlike) *comes by grace through faith*. In Colossians 2:6-7, Paul urges, "So then, just as you received Christ Jesus as Lord, continue to live your lives in him, rooted and built up in him, strengthened in the faith as you were taught, and overflowing with thankfulness."

The fact that our sanctification is God's work and comes to us by grace through faith does not relieve us of responsibility however. This gets at the *diligence* side of the equation. God has given us the *following skills* as tools, resources and strategies by which we can deepen our relationship with Him. As we diligently pursue an ever-deepening relationship with Christ through the *following skills*, He changes us.

The Apostle Paul draws attention to this dependence and diligence in Philippians 2:12-13, "Continue to work out your salvation with fear and trembling *[the diligence]*, for it is God who works in you to will and to act in order to fulfill his good purpose *[the dependence]*." Jesus' command for us to "abide in," or "remain in" Him also illustrates this dependent-diligence. (John 15:4)

The Apostle Peter alludes to this dependent-diligence in 2 Peter 1:3 (NLT). There he says, "By his divine power, God has given us everything we need for living a godly life." This shows our complete *dependence* on God for living a godly life. Then, in verse 5 he continues, "In view of all this, *make every effort* to respond to God's promises." Here he identifies our *diligence* in responding to God.

Also, this pivotal principle of dependent-diligence is not a balancing act between the two. Instead, we are to be totally dependent on Christ and fervently diligent in pursuing Him.

The fifth pivotal principle states that *spiritual transformation requires both dependence and diligence*.

To sum up, a disciple of Jesus Christ actively and intentionally pursues *relationship* with Jesus by spending time with Him and getting to know Him better. We do that in great measure by exercising the *following skills* like prayer and reading God's Word. Pursuing an ever-deepening relationship with Christ requires *diligence* on our part, but as we saw from the vine and branches metaphor, we are totally *dependent* on Christ for producing "fruit" or godliness in our lives.

Let's review these five pivotal principles:

- Our primary goal is to cultivate an ever-deepening relationship with Jesus Christ
- Our spiritual transformation *results from* our relationship with Christ

- The purpose of the *following skills* is to help us know Christ better
- Evidence of spiritual maturity is *Christlikeness*, not how much or how well we practice the *following skills*
- Spiritual transformation is a life-long process that requires both dependence and diligence

Discussion Questions

1. Explain why the author argues that godliness must not be our primary goal. Do you agree with the author's position on this? Why or why not?

2. Why is knowing Christ more deeply our primary goal? See Philippians 3:8-11.

3. Discuss your relationship with Christ in light of John 15:5.

4. How does godliness result from abiding in or remaining in Christ?

5. Describe a situation in which you used a *following skill* in an attempt to impress God or others rather than assist you in knowing Him better.

6. What is the true measure of spiritual maturity and why?

7. In what way is God speaking to you from this chapter? What will you do as a result?

8. Pray with and for each other. We will go over the guidelines of praying with others in chapter 5, but for now simply follow these practices as you pray with each other:

- Pray *short*, phrase or sentence prayers (Don't hog the conversation!)
- Listen to the Holy Spirit and each other
- Piggyback on each other's prayers. Stay on a theme until it seems right to move on
- Keep your prayers vertical (God-ward)
- Embrace silence as an opportunity to listen to God, transition to another topic, or process what has been prayed
- Believe the best of each other

ON ALERT!

– Chapter 2 –

CALL TO ACTION

Be alert and always keep on praying. Ephesians 6:18

Pray and stay alert!

During the Cold War, I was drafted into the US Army and volunteered for a third year. On more than one occasion during my three-year term of service, the US military was placed on alert. One of the most memorable incidents that put us on alert was the 1973 Yom Kippur attack by Egypt and Syria on our ally Israel. This incident was especially significant for those of us who were stationed in Europe at the time.

While on alert we maintained a state of heightened readiness, watchfulness, and constant communication. We put on our field gear, made certain our combat equipment was in order and at hand, all leave was canceled, and we were ready to deploy at a moment's notice. Our minds were sharpened and focused to anticipate whatever might come our way while on alert.

In much the same way, Jesus Christ has put us on alert until He returns. Jesus urges His disciples (including us) to "be on the alert," "keep watch," and "be ready." Catch the urgency and gravity of Jesus' words in the following passages:

> *Therefore **be on the alert**, for you do not know which day your Lord is coming. – Matthew 24:42 (NASB)*

> *So you also must **be ready**, because the Son of Man will come at an hour when you do not expect him. – Matthew 24:44*

> *Therefore **keep watch**, because you do not know the day or the hour. – Matthew 25:13*

> ***Watch** and pray so that you will not fall into temptation. The spirit is willing, but the flesh is weak. – Matthew 26:41*

> *It will be good for those servants whose*
> *master finds them **watching** when he*
> *comes. – Luke 12:37*

To the above passages, the Apostle Peter adds, "**Be alert** and of sober mind. Your enemy the devil prowls around like a roaring lion looking for someone to devour." (1 Peter 5:8)

What does *being on alert* look like for a follower of Christ today? In Ephesians 6 where the Apostle Paul warns us to "be strong in the Lord and in His mighty power," he gives us at least one primary aspect of maintaining a vigilant stance. Paul urges, "And **pray** in the Spirit on all occasions **with all kinds of prayers** and requests. With this in mind, be alert and always **keep on praying**...." (Ephesians 6:18)

The Apostle Peter also tightly links prayer with staying on the alert. "The end of all things is near. Therefore be alert and of sober mind so that you may **pray**." (1 Peter 4:7)

Our Commander 'n Chief, our Lord Jesus Christ has put us *on alert*. One of the primary ways we maintain our vigilance is through prayer—constant communication—with Him. But often, it seems, we lose our sense of urgency. We forget what we're about as followers of Jesus. We find ourselves more *distracted* than *alert*.

Sometimes our lives bear down on us to the extent that we lose heart.

Pray and do not lose heart

In Luke 18:1, we read that Jesus told His disciples "a parable to the effect that they ought always to pray and not lose heart." (ESV) The NIV renders the verse, "Then Jesus told his disciples a parable to show them that they should always pray and not give up." The parable Jesus tells here offers us some powerful truths and instructions about prayer:

> And he told them a parable to the effect that they ought always to pray and not lose heart. ² He said, "In a certain city there was a judge who neither feared God nor respected man. ³ And there was a widow in that city who kept coming to him and saying, 'Give me justice against my adversary.'
>
> ⁴ For a while he refused, but afterward he said to himself, 'Though I neither fear God nor respect man, ⁵ yet because this widow keeps bothering me, I will give her justice, so that she will not beat me down by her continual coming.'"
>
> ⁶ And the Lord said, "Hear what the unrighteous judge says. ⁷ And will not

34

God give justice to his elect, who cry to him day and night? Will he delay long over them? [8] I tell you, he will give justice to them speedily. Nevertheless, when the Son of Man comes, will he find faith on earth?" (Luke 18:1-8 ESV)

Let's see what we can learn from this parable. I see two primary takeaways. First, *pray persistently*. We must always pray and not lose heart—never give up. Anything worth praying about is worth praying for *fervently* and *persistently*. The widow in the story exemplifies this persistence and perseverance. Never ever give up! Paul urged the Thessalonians to "Pray without ceasing." (1 Thessalonians 5:17 ESV)

Praying persistently means to pray with *courage*—"do not lose heart!" In other words, "Don't be a wuss! Keep on praying!" In Ephesians 6:10, Paul challenges us to "Be strong in the Lord and in his mighty power." Then he tells us to put on the armor of God. Finishing up with that list of equipment, Paul adds, "And pray in the Spirit on all occasions with all kinds of prayers and requests. With this in mind, be alert and always keep on praying for all the Lord's people." (Ephesians 6:18)

Some might be thinking right now, "If God is all-knowing, why do I have to pray at all? And specifically why must I *persevere* in prayer? Didn't God hear me the first time?"

I believe the second takeaway from this parable helps explain these questions.

The second significant takeaway is to *pray expectantly*. Praying expectantly is based on two premises: 1) God's holy and loving character; and, 2) our trust in Him as such. In this parable, Jesus tells about an unjust, mean, and crooked judge. Jesus uses the example of the unjust judge to *contrast* what God is really like.

Unlike this judge, God *does care* about us; He loves us; He stands for justice; He cannot be bribed; He judges rightly; He is never annoyed by our coming to Him; and He responds quickly. (Justice happens to be the widow's request in the story, but God is eager to answer all our prayers.)

The Bible is very clear about God's character. He is pure, loving and holy. The question is whether we believe that and trust Him. I believe this is why Jesus closes the parable with the question, "Nevertheless, when the Son of Man comes, will he find faith on earth?"

These two premises for expectant prayer, the character of God, coupled with our faith, are also found in Hebrews 11:6. "And without faith it is impossible to please God, because anyone who comes to him must believe that he exists and that he rewards those who earnestly seek him." We come to God in prayer expectantly, *believing* that He is able *and* willing to answer our prayers.

James 1:5-8 also teaches on this point of expectant prayer, but is often misunderstood.

> *If any of you lacks wisdom, let him ask God, who gives generously to all without reproach, and it will be given him. ⁶ But let him ask in faith, with no doubting, for the one who doubts is like a wave of the sea that is driven and tossed by the wind. ⁷ For that person must not suppose that he will receive anything from the Lord; ⁸ he is a double-minded man, unstable in all his ways. (ESV)*

In this passage, James is talking about wisdom and the fact that we can freely ask God for it. Again, wisdom is not the only thing we can ask for, it just happens to be the subject of this prayer. Notice that James also includes those two premises for expectant prayer: God's generous and unbiased character and our faith in Him as such.

Where we get sidetracked in this passage is the part about doubting: "But let him ask in faith, with no doubting." James is not referring to the strength or integrity of our faith, but to the *object* of our faith—holy God. In other words, if we pray to God, but doubt His holy character or loving intentions, then we might as well not have prayed!

A person who prays but doubts God's character will be "like a wave of the sea that is driven and tossed by the wind." They have no solid ground to stand on. They're "double-minded, unstable in all their ways." After all, why would we pray to a god who can't or won't help us?

Back to those two questions I posed earlier, "If God is all-knowing then why do I need to pray at all? And, why especially would I have to persevere in prayer?" We pray because prayer is communication—communion with our Lord. If we are in relationship with Him, our relationship requires two-way communication. Prayer is a core element of that.

Also, He wants us to live dependently on Him. He wants us to trust that He is good and that we can expect Him to answer. Trust is not one of those things about which we can say, "I did that." Trust or faith is a way of life in which we are totally dependent on Christ day by day, moment by moment. Prayer is an everyday expression of our trust and dependence on Christ. Ceasing to trust or pray is not an option for the Christ-follower. Believing prayer is our way of life in Christ.

Coming full circle, we must pray *persistently* and pray *expectantly*. We have a great God! We have a loving heavenly Father who delights in hearing from us and in answering our prayers!

> I love the Lord, for he heard my voice; he heard my cry for mercy. Because he turned his ear to me, I will call on him as long as I live. – Psalm 116:1-2

So far, we've seen that Jesus has put us on alert and one of the chief ways we maintain our watchful stance is in prayer. We also recognize that we need to persevere in prayer no matter what, believing expectantly that our heavenly Father will answer us. There's yet another key component of prayer that we must not overlook—prayer is especially significant in the life and work of the leader.

Prayer – a core practice of leaders

The fact that prayer is a core leadership practice is so obvious that we're liable to miss the trees for the forest. There may well be dozens of reasons why prayer is so crucial for the leader in leading others, but I will limit the reasons I give here to seven.

First, God tells us how vital prayer is. If we don't get that as leaders, our leadership is doomed. In Paul's first letter to Timothy, Paul wrote Timothy so that he and the followers of Christ under his care would know how to conduct themselves in the church—God's household (1 Timothy 3:14-15).

Then, in chapter 2, verse 1, Paul leads out, "I urge then, first of all, that petitions, prayers, intercession and thanksgiving be made for all people." Paul uses the phrase, "first of all," to indicate the urgency and primacy he places on prayer. Prayer is clearly a vital and urgent practice that leaders must vision and model for others.

Second, prayer is a core leadership practice demonstrated by our Lord Jesus. Luke comments, "But Jesus often withdrew to lonely places and prayed." (Luke 5:16) And Hebrews 5:7 records, "During the days of Jesus' life on earth, he offered up prayers and petitions with fervent cries and tears to the one who could save him from death, and he was heard because of his reverent submission."

There can be no doubt that Jesus is our model for leadership and that prayer was a core practice of His. We must follow His lead. If Jesus, the Son of God sensed an urgent need to remain in constant communication with the Father, then how much more must we?

Third, prayer is also a core leadership practice demonstrated by every other primary leader in the Scriptures. From Abraham, Moses, Joshua, Samuel, David, Jeremiah, Daniel, Ezra and Nehemiah in the Old Testament we see men who were strong leaders and who modeled prayer.

We see the same in the New Testament in the lives of Paul, Peter, John and the other apostles and followers of Christ. Of the early church Luke wrote, "They devoted themselves...to prayer." (Acts 2:42) Even when other very important matters threatened to distract the apostles they recognized the need to delegate those responsibilities to others so they could "give their attention to prayer and the ministry of the word." (Acts 6:4) If we aspire to lead others, we too must pray.

Fourth, prayer demonstrates our allegiance to and dependence on Christ as our Leader. All leadership flows from a higher authority, except with God Himself. As leaders, we must remain in constant communication with our Commander and Chief. How can we possibly lead others for Christ without His direction, wisdom and strength? Nehemiah, facing severe opposition to the difficult work of rebuilding the walls of Jerusalem, constantly turned to God in prayer: "But I prayed, 'Now strengthen my hands.'" (Nehemiah 6:9)

Fifth, prayer must be a core practice in our lives as leaders because we too must model prayer for others. Someone who says one thing, but does another is called a *hypocrite*. Surely we ourselves see the need to pray. As leaders we must share our passion for prayer with others by leading them in prayer. When others see our devotion to Christ in prayer, they too will pray.

Sixth, leadership is primarily about character. We may have all the other leadership qualities, but without character we cannot lead well. Christlike character is built in the presence of Christ. Prayer brings us into His presence. We pray, "Your kingdom come, your will be done, on earth as it is in heaven." (Matthew 6:10) "Lord, we invite You to transform us and make us like You in character."

Seventh, prayer is a core practice of leaders, because leaders lead through vision and vision comes through prayer. Bill Hybels calls vision "A leader's most potent weapon."[4] Then he defines vision as "A picture of the future that produces passion."[5] But where does vision come from? Obviously, if vision is a picture of the future, you and I don't have that insight. But God does. In prayer, He reveals to us what He sees and desires for us and those we lead.

When Solomon was crowned king of Israel, he prayed to God:

> *Now, Lord my God, you have made your servant king in place of my father David. But I am only a little child and do not know how to carry out my duties.[8] Your servant is here among the people you have chosen, a great people, too numerous to count or number. [9] So give your servant a discerning heart to govern*

> *your people and to distinguish between*
> *right and wrong. For who is able to*
> *govern this great people of yours? (1*
> *Kings 3:7-9)*

Prayer is a core practice of leaders. May we learn to excel at prayer, so that we may excel at leading others.

The worst sin

The Scottish theologian P. T. Forsyth wrote, "The worst sin is prayerlessness."[6] By that statement he did NOT mean that when we do not pray we have failed to fulfill our *duty* to a commandment of God. Instead, what Forsyth was getting at is that "the root of all sin is self-sufficiency—independence from God."[7] Sin is going our own way, rather than God's way. When we fail to pray, we rely on our own wisdom, strength and resources instead of on God's.

In Psalm 53:4, David lists one of the chief characteristics of "evildoers." He laments that "They never call on God." Prayer squelches our tendency toward independence. Prayer demonstrates a humble admission of dependence on God. Prayer knocks self-sufficiency on its butt!

As men, we struggle with this whole concept. We tend to see ourselves as self-sufficient and independent. We laud the "self-made man." It's as though we men were bred to need no one. But our self-sufficiency translates into self-centeredness, an unhealthy independence, and even rebellion. "Look out for number one!" With this mindset is it any wonder we fail at relationships and struggle with prayer?

Self-sufficiency is our undoing. Independence and going it on our own is at the heart of all sin. This is what Jesus died to save us from. We acknowledge our sin and demonstrate our desperate need for God in prayer. Through prayer we come to Him, fellowship with Him and trust Him with our lives.

As Jesus instructed His disciples in the Garden of Gethsemane, so He instructs us to "Watch and pray so that you will not fall into temptation. The spirit is willing, but the flesh is weak." (Matthew 26:41)

Practice

If you're not already doing so, please set aside time to get alone and pray each day. Whatever else you pray for or about, make sure you come to prayer simply praising, thanking and enjoying the Lord's presence. Practice listening more than talking. Don't be a clock-watcher in your prayer time. If you are new at this, set a very achievable goal of spending five or ten minutes alone with the Lord.

Discussion Questions

1. What is the correlation between prayer and staying alert as we follow Christ? What does it mean to be "watchful" in prayer?

2. What are the primary barriers for you in terms of praying persistently? When do you tend to lose heart in prayer?

3. On what two principles is praying expectantly based? Why are both of these principles so vital?

4. Explain Hebrews 11:6. In what way can you apply this passage specifically in your life right now?

5. Discuss at least three reasons why prayer must be a core practice of leaders. How does this impact you personally?

6. Why is a self-sufficient attitude the enemy of prayer?

7. In the Practice portion of this chapter, you were asked to establish a specific time each day to pray with the Lord. How is that going? What has been positive about your time with the Lord? What do you find challenging? Ask a spiritual partner to pray for you in this regard.

8. Pray with and for each other. We will go over the guidelines of praying with others in chapter 5, but for now simply follow these practices as you pray with each other:

    • Pray *short*, phrase or sentence prayers (Don't hog the conversation!)
    • Listen to the Holy Spirit and each other

- Piggyback on each other's prayers. Stay on a theme until it seems right to move on
- Keep your prayers vertical (God-ward)
- Embrace silence as an opportunity to listen to God, transition to another topic, or process what has been prayed
- Believe the best of each other

---

[4] Bill Hybels, *Courageous Leadership*, (Grand Rapids, MI: Zondervan, 2002), p. 29.

[5] Bill Hybels, p. 32.

[6] P. T. Forsyth, *Soul of Prayer*, CreateSpace Independent Publishing Platform, 2013, p. 1.

[7] Charles E. Hummel, *Tyranny of the Urgent*, (Downers Grove, IL: Inter-Varsity Press, 1967), p. 10.

— Chapter 3 —

WHAT IS PRAYER?

You who answer prayer, to you all people will come.
Psalm 65:2

Two-way communication is essential to any relationship

While in the military during the Cold War, I received a very unique job assignment in West Berlin, Germany. The Army trained me as a German linguist so I could analyze East German military radio transmissions. Communications are one of the most strategic factors on the battlefield. Intercept or disrupt enemy communications and you've got a tremendous edge over the enemy.

The same holds true in a marriage relationship. "Communication is to a relationship what blood is to the human body. Communication nourishes and sustains a relationship. Remove it and you no longer have a relationship."[8] If you're married, you have no doubt experienced what happens when you and your spouse find yourselves in a season of non-communication. Your imaginations run amok and your relationship begins to disintegrate.

We could go on about the pivotal role of communication in business, church, politics, sports teams, family, and every other relationship we can think of. Communication is central to any relationship. In fact, *without two-way communication a relationship cannot exist.*[9]

Prayer is our communication link with God. Is it any wonder that the evil one would like nothing better than to disrupt our communications with God? If our communication with the Father is interrupted, our relationship is jeopardized.

One of the chief schemes of the devil is to confuse us about prayer, because of the vital role it plays in our relationship with Christ. As a result, many Christians have developed very flawed ideas about prayer. I know because I've been there myself. Let me describe a scene for you that illustrates my struggle with prayer when I was a young man.

Misconceptions about prayer

When my wife and I got married I was in the Army stationed in West Berlin, Germany. We lived in a tiny newly-wed nest in the finished half of an attic. The other half of the attic was an unheated, unfinished storage area.

At the time, I had been reading biographies of great men and women of God and was especially moved by their exemplary prayer lives. By contrast, my prayer life looked pathetic! I set about to change all that.

My brilliant plan was to get up at 4 am and quietly slip out of our apartment and into the unfinished, unheated portion of the attic. To complete my rigorous regimen, I knelt on the cold stone pavers of the attic floor (yes, the attic floor was actually paved with stone bricks) and rested my elbows on a hard wooden apple crate.

Even in my youth, this was terribly uncomfortable and unpleasant, but I actually thought at the time that such self-abasement and suffering would aid in my attempts to become a great man of prayer.

The first day or two of this pious regimen went reasonably well, but slid quickly downhill from there. The combination of the early morning rise and the cold, dark attic were the perfect recipe for sleep—though not a very restful one.

I was tough on myself for falling asleep while praying and felt increasingly less spiritual because of it. I had really thought that getting up early and praying would make me feel *more* spiritual! I couldn't figure out what was going wrong. Though by rights I should have been becoming more holy than my slumbering wife, it irritated me to no end that she would rise hours later so cheerfully after a good night's sleep.

The final nail in the coffin of my prayer experiment drove home when my loving wife confronted me one day while I was throwing a fit. She accurately pointed out that my very early mornings, the severities of my prayer chamber and the guilt I laid on myself in my failure all collaborated to make me very grumpy and difficult to live with!

Unfortunately, I walked away from my failed prayer experiment in Berlin resigned to a life of mediocre communication with God. "I must not have the knack for prayer," I thought.

In fairness to myself and others who may relate to my failure, I was young and inexperienced in my relationship with God. I also had some major paradigm shifts to make regarding a proper understanding and application of the *following skills* like prayer.

The list of distorted prayer concepts is long. Jesus corrected at least two misconceptions in the Sermon on the Mount when He warned us *not* to pray, "Like the hypocrites, for they love to pray...that they may be seen by others." Then He added, "And when you pray, do not heap up empty phrases as the Gentiles do, for they think that they will be heard for their many words." (Matthew 6:5-7 ESV)

Some view prayer like an incantation requiring a specific formula for it to work. A short time ago I heard a Christian man suggest that for God to hear us we must observe the *right* posture and speak the *right* words. *Really?*

Others treat God like a genie in a lamp. They come to Him in prayer, "rub the lamp" and expect Him to perform for them. Such an approach sees prayer primarily as a means of asking God for stuff, or getting Him to do something He would not have done otherwise. Still others view prayer as a contractual agreement. If they meet certain conditions, they think God is *obligated* to meet their demands.

Another commonly held but flawed view of prayer is that it is *one-way* communication. "I talk; God listens." Imagine what would happen if I suggested to my wife the following: "Honey, from now on, we'll communicate with each other each morning at 6 am. We'll meet for 20 minutes. I'll do all the talking and all you have to do is listen."

Such an arrangement would be laughable! How can we think that two-way communication is any less important in our relationship with God? Two-way communication is vital to any relationship including our relationship with God.

Distorted views of prayer demean and belittle our holy, awesome God, destroy our communication with Him, and stunt our growth in Christ. With so much confusion about prayer we might wonder, "Is prayer really that difficult and complicated?" No, it is not!

Many years ago, I was discipling a young man named Steve. Steve was a new follower of Christ and like many men, found it difficult to pray out loud with others. Even when the two of us were the only ones in the room, he could not bring himself to pray out loud. I could tell that his fear also inhibited his private prayer with God.

I prayed that God would give him the freedom to pray with others. In addition to my prayer, I invited Steve to dinner one night, but I had a secret agenda. When we all sat down at the dinner table, I casually asked our four-year-old son, Jason, if he would say grace for us. Jason spontaneously prayed a beautiful four-year-old's prayer and we ate.

After supper, Steve and I retreated downstairs to spend time in our Bible study together. But before I could begin, Steve blurted out, "I am so humbled by your son's prayer! If a little kid can pray out loud like that, then so can I! Can we pray right now?" So we did. Steve prayed for the first time out loud in the company of someone else. A few lines into his prayer he looked up at me and asked, "How am I doing?" I laughed and told him he was doing great, not to worry about what I thought, and to continue. Today, Steve pastors a church and teaches others how to pray.

All three of our children and all of our grandchildren started praying as soon as they could talk. Prayer is neither difficult nor complex. In the next chapter we'll look at the simplicity of prayer. But for now let me whet your appetite with some examples of answered prayer from my life.

God answers prayer

After serving in the military, my wife and I landed in Spokane, Washington believing that the Lord was leading us to go to Bible College and eventually become missionaries overseas. Linda was pregnant, and we had no medical insurance due to the fact that her pregnancy was a pre-existing condition. Two months before her due date, she was diagnosed with preeclampsia and the doctor confined her to bed for the duration of her pregnancy.

We had just moved into an apartment in Spokane and didn't know a soul for we had never lived here before. The costs of establishing our new household and all that entails, coupled with unexpectedly having to replace the transmission in our car, left us penniless. We could not even afford a phone, so I made daily treks to a phone booth about a block away as I looked for a job. On the way to the phone booth, I would pray for a dime to make each call. Consistently, the Lord provided a dime on the sidewalk, in the coin return, or on the floor of the phone booth. We were really that broke!

One day during those two months we received a sizeable doctor bill in the mail. We laid it out on the bed and prayed together that God would provide. The next day, we received an anonymous cashier's check in the mail for the *exact amount—to the penny* of that doctor bill. We had not mentioned the bill to anyone. In fact, we still didn't know anyone we could've mentioned it to, but God had answered our prayer. To this day, we have no idea who could have sent that check.

On another occasion during those difficult days, we needed to fill a prescription that Linda was to take, but we had no money. Again, I sat down on the bed next to her and we prayed that God would provide. As soon as we said, "Amen", I sensed the Lord prompting me to go to the pharmacy and pick up her prescription. I know that sounds crazy, but I had a clear leading of the Lord to go to the store and watch Him provide.

So I told Linda what I was doing and drove to the store. As I swung open the door of the car to get out, I looked down on the ground and there was a big pile of change. I hadn't noticed it when I drove in. I was amazed and humbled! I scooped it all up and walked into the store quite certain that it would cover the cost of the prescription. It did!

I could go on and on telling you about how God has answered very specific prayers for the past 39 years of our marriage. In fact, the ones I've shared with you here are "small" in comparison with others He has answered more recently. But those answers to prayer are still fresh and very meaningful to me because God was building our trust in Him with every dime He provided.

Those answers to prayer were so immediate and so tangible. His answers are not always like that. At times we needed to learn how to *persist* in prayer and wait on the Lord, still trusting that He heard us, cared about us, and would eventually answer us based on His sovereign design.

Years later, when Linda and I were missionaries in Austria, we had befriended a local store owner and his wife. For Mother's Day, we invited them to our little church in Baden and then out to dinner afterward. Ours was a small church, so during the service we enjoyed hearing people in the congregation share what God had been doing in their lives all week. This particular Sunday, perhaps a half dozen folks shared. Their interactions with God were very personal and tender, but they reported nothing that we might call sensational.

Afterward at lunch, we asked our unsaved friends what they thought of the service. Immediately, our friends became very judgmental and derided our sharing time at church. Our friends spat out their ridicule venomously, "Who do those people think they are that Almighty God would care about their petty little issues!?"

At the time, I didn't have an answer for them, but went home and asked the Lord for His response. I found it in 1 Peter 5:6-7 (ESV), "Humble yourselves, therefore, under the mighty hand of God so that at the proper time he may exalt you, casting all your anxieties on him, because he cares for you."

While our friends viewed taking our "petty issues" to God in prayer as *prideful*, God actually shows us that doing so is the path to *humility*. God says, "Humble yourselves…." How? By "casting all your anxieties on him, because he cares for you." Coming to God in prayer is always the humble, God-honoring thing to do. Our friends' wrong thinking also begs the question, "Who invented prayer anyway? God or mankind?" Let's look at the basis for prayer to find out.

The basis for prayer

As far back as Genesis 3, God has always been the initiator to bring us into relationship with Him. He is the one who put things in motion to mend the rift in our relationships caused by sin. He is the one who urges us to "Seek the Lord" (Deuteronomy 4:29; Isaiah 55:6). He invented prayer and invites us to commune with Him (Jeremiah 33:3). In fact, for us today the basis for prayer is Christ and His reconciling work on our behalf.

Hebrews 4:14-16 provides a great explanation for how and why we can approach God in prayer:

> *Therefore, since we have a great high priest who has ascended into heaven, Jesus the Son of God, let us hold firmly to the faith we profess. For we do not have a high priest who is unable to empathize with our weaknesses, but we have one who has been tempted in every way, just as we are—yet he did not sin. Let us then approach God's throne of grace with confidence, so that we may receive mercy and find grace to help us in our time of need.*

Through Jesus Christ and His priestly work on our behalf, we can "approach God's throne of grace with confidence." Christ accomplished this for us when He paid the penalty for our sins on the cross and opened the way for us to go directly to the Father. Jesus reconciled us to the Father, not only forgiving us, but making us His children. This point is hugely important!

What wouldn't any of us fathers do for our children? Not only do we love our kids, care for their needs, and lavish good things on them, but we would lay down our lives for them. In the context of that thought, Jesus countered, "If you, then, though you are evil, know how to give good gifts to your children, how much more will your Father in heaven give good gifts to those who ask Him!" (Matthew 7:11)

Grasping this truth is fundamental to prayer. Your heavenly Father loves you so much as His son, that He "sent the Spirit of His Son into our hearts, the Spirit who calls out, 'Abba, Father.'" (Galatians 4:6) Abba is Aramaic for "Daddy". You may not have grown up with a godly model for a dad, but don't make the mistake of transferring that image onto your heavenly Father. "He [God] who did not spare his own Son, but gave him up for us all—how will he not also, along with him, graciously give us all things?" (Romans 8:32)

By faith in Jesus Christ and His death, burial and resurrection, we stand holy and blameless before the Father. He receives us as His sons. He is a proud and doting Father who wants to lavish His kindness upon us. Nothing stands between us and Him. Jesus has cleared the way. Jesus' work on our behalf establishes the basis for prayer.

In 1 Timothy 2:1 & 5, Paul wrote, "I urge, then, first of all, that petitions, prayers, intercession and thanksgiving be made for all people—for there is one God and one mediator between God and mankind, the man Christ Jesus." Our Lord Jesus Christ establishes the basis for prayer. Through faith in Him we can boldly approach the Father.

Life-changing prayer

Prayer is simply and primarily *communion* with God. Prayer, like all the following skills, chiefly serves to help us draw closer to Christ. In Christ's presence we are transformed. Therefore, in a very real sense, *prayer is a conversation with God in which we align ourselves with Him, His character and purposes.*

In his book, *Celebration of Discipline*, Richard Foster writes, "To pray is to change. Prayer is the central avenue God uses to transform us."[10] That statement may challenge our thinking, but remember what we concluded earlier. In Jesus' presence we are transformed. *As we draw near to God, we cannot remain unchanged*. When we pray, we are drawing near to God. Prayer ushers us into His presence. In this way, prayer is our path to life change, because it leads us into His presence.

Notice that this is how Jesus modeled prayer for his disciples. He said:

> *This, then, is how you should pray: "Our Father in heaven, hallowed be your name, your kingdom come, your will be done on earth as it is in heaven. Give us today our daily bread. Forgive us our debts, as we also have forgiven our debtors. And lead us not into temptation, but deliver us from the evil one." (Matthew 6:9-13)*

Look back over the words of this model prayer that Jesus gave us. The Lord invites us to a very *personal* interaction with Him as *Father* even though He is the high and exalted One: "Our Father in heaven." We acknowledge God's holiness and *desire* His rule in our lives just as surely as He reigns over all of heaven: "Hallowed be your name, your kingdom come, your will be done on earth as it is in heaven."

We continue by acknowledging that everything we need comes from Him and that He wants to meet our needs, so we ask Him freely for them: "Give us today our daily bread." We then humble ourselves admitting and confessing to Him our sins. And we do so with a clear conscience that we too have extended mercy and forgiveness toward others who have sinned against us:

"Forgive us our debts, as we also have forgiven our debtors."

Finally, we own up to our weakness and propensity toward sin and ask Him to lead us out of temptation and to protect us from the evil one. In so praying, we knowingly set a course for our lives that shuns and avoids what would grieve and displease our Lord: "And lead us not into temptation, but deliver us from the evil one." This prayer is intensely personal and yearns for God to do His life-changing work in us.

Let's investigate this life-changing aspect of prayer a bit further. In 1 Peter 2:11, Peter urges us to "abstain from sinful desires." My longing (and I'm sure yours too) is for God to take those sinful desires from me and exchange them for His pure desires. In prayer we seek to align our desires with God's. Jesus prayed in the Garden of Gethsemane, "Not my will but yours be done." (Matthew 26:39)

However, as long as we're in the flesh, we will do battle with sinful desires. Yet we are still to *abstain* or *refrain* from giving in to them. We are often so weak in this regard—not only because our desires can be so strong— but because it's so natural (in the flesh) to give in to them. But we don't have to! That's what it means to pray, "Your will be done on earth as it is in heaven."

In the Garden on the night He was betrayed, Jesus urged His disciples to watch and pray so that they wouldn't yield to temptation. He put them on alert. He offered them prayer on the darkest night in history as a means for counter-acting their human inclination to give in to temptation.

I find it incredibly helpful to converse with God about my sinful desires. He already knows I'm struggling with them anyway. By talking to Him about them it all comes out in the open and makes it easier to deal with. But often we behave like Adam when he sinned and tried to hide himself from God. Like Adam, we're embarrassed and ashamed so we ignore (hide) the desire instead of confronting it, even though God knows our every thought and desires.

Next time you find yourself entertaining fleshly desires about lust, or greed, or anger, or...(fill in the blank), talk to God about it. Tell Him something like this, "Lord, as you know, I'm really struggling right now with lust. I know it's neither right nor healthy. Please transform me and make me pure. I want my desires to be aligned with Yours. I denounce these evil desires and the wicked behaviors they could spawn. I want to be more like You, Jesus!"

After praying like that (this is very important!) *take the next step*—walk away from whatever was feeding that desire. "Put feet to your prayers." Just walk away from that fleshly desire! Many times we make the mistake of waiting for our desires to change first then we obey. That's not living by faith. We've *prayed*, now we *act*.

Although Jesus was sinless, He modeled this pattern for us in the garden. He *prayed*, "Not my will but yours be done." Then He *acted*, "Rise! Let us go! Here comes my betrayer!" Jesus didn't run and cower behind a tree. He got up and went to meet His accusers. He went willingly to the mob that had come out to arrest Him. *Pray*, and then *act* in faith according to your prayer.

Prayer is conversation with God in which we align ourselves with Him, His character and purposes.

Practice

What is one thing you'd like to see Christ change in you right now? This may be a sinful pattern, or a character issue. Pray each day regarding this thing. Tell God you want to move it out of your life and replace it with Christlikeness. Engage the prayers of a spiritual partner or comrade in arms to help you beat this thing.

Discussion Questions

1. Describe the role of communication (prayer) in our relationship with God.

2. In what ways can you relate to Rob's early attempts at prayer? What specific aspects of prayer have you struggled with in the past or present?

3. Rob mentions a number of distorted concepts of prayer. Which of these came as a surprise to you? What other prayer practices can you think of that are unbiblical?

4. Discuss your own journey with prayer. How would you describe prayer in terms of its difficulty or complexity?

5. Why is prayer so central to our spiritual transformation (becoming more Christlike)?

6. In what ways is the Lord's Prayer so transformational?

7. Discuss how Jesus prepared the way for us to be able to pray.

8. Why does prayer play such a crucial role in dealing with sin in our lives?

9. Describe what your prayer looks like with the Lord today. What have you found works best for you and what doesn't work?

10. Pray with and for each other. We will go over the guidelines of praying with others in chapter 5, but for now simply follow these practices as you pray with each other:

- Pray *short*, phrase or sentence prayers (Don't hog the conversation!)
- Listen to the Holy Spirit and each other
- Piggyback on each other's prayers. Stay on a theme until it seems right to move on
- Keep your prayers vertical (God-ward)
- Embrace silence as an opportunity to listen to God, transition to another topic, or process what has been prayed
- Believe the best of each other

---

[8] David Boehi, et al, *Preparing for Marriage*, (Ventura, CA: Gospel Light, 1997), p. 139.

[9] I cover this in greater detail in my book, *Enthralled with God*.

[10] Richard Foster, *Celebration of Discipline*, (New York: HarperCollins Publishers, 1978), p. 33.

– Chapter 4 –

HOW TO PRAY

Lord, teach us to pray. Luke 11:1

Teach us to pray

"One day Jesus was praying in a certain place. When he finished, one of his disciples said to him, 'Lord, teach us to pray, just as John taught his disciples.'" (Luke 11:1) Let's unpack this passage and see what was going on here.

First, we notice that Jesus modeled a life of prayer before His disciples. Earlier in Luke 5:16, Luke comments, "Jesus often withdrew to lonely places and prayed." And in Luke 9:18 we read, "Once when Jesus was praying in private and his disciples were with him…." Also in Luke 9:28 we find, "About eight days after Jesus said this, he took Peter, John and James with him and went up onto a mountain to pray." And finally, in Luke 11:1 we read, "One day Jesus was praying…."

Clearly, prayer was a core element of Jesus' life. He was constantly in communion with His Father and His disciples witnessed this first-hand. But Jesus' example is meant for us as well. His disciples passed on this legacy of prayer to their disciples, and so on. Now this prayer legacy has been passed on to us.

Second, Jesus modeled prayer in a way that His disciples found *desirable*. "Lord, teach us to pray…" is a heartfelt request that came after His disciples observed Him praying. "Lord, we want to be like You. We long to know the Father like You know Him. *Please teach us to pray*."

When Jesus prayed, men *longed* to pray like Him. What have *we* made prayer that causes men to *avoid* it? (I'll say more about this in the next chapter.)

Third, Jesus' disciples asked Him to teach them to pray, "Just as John taught his disciples." This is a reference to John the Baptist. This underscores the fact that prayer is a learned skill and that this skill is central to discipleship. To a great extent we learn to pray through the example of other followers of Christ and from the Lord Himself.

And for good or for bad, others will also learn to pray from watching and listening to you and me.

Finally, when the disciples asked Jesus to teach them to pray, He responded, "Pray like this." (Matthew 6:9 NLT) And then He role-played a model prayer for them.

We've already looked at the model prayer that Jesus gave His disciples, but let's discuss it once more with a different focus. I'll use Matthew's version because it's more complete:

> This, then, is how you should pray: "Our Father in heaven, hallowed be your name, your kingdom come, your will be done, on earth as it is in heaven. Give us today our daily bread. And forgive us our debts, as we also have forgiven our debtors. And lead us not into temptation, but deliver us from the evil one." (Matthew 6:9-13)

Notice some of the elements of this prayer. This prayer includes praise; an expressed longing for God's Kingdom to be established and His will to be done; a request for our daily needs; asking forgiveness while affirming that we've forgiven others; and finally a request for protection from temptation and the evil one. Lastly, notice how short this prayer is. I hope you find that as freeing as I do. Jesus' model prayer was short and to the point.

Let's look at some other prayers that God included for us in His Word, so that we might learn to pray.

Nehemiah was a Jewish man who was conscripted by King Artaxerxes to serve as his cupbearer in Babylon. The Jews had been in captivity for the past 70 years because of their sin. Recently some Jews had been allowed to return to Israel and rebuild the temple in Jerusalem. But the city wall was broken down and its gates burned. Enemies near Jerusalem were harassing the Jews there and hindering the work. Nehemiah received word of their condition from one of his brothers and recorded the following:

> When I heard these things, I sat down and wept. For some days I mourned and fasted and prayed before the God of heaven. Then I said:
>
> "Lord, the God of heaven, the great and awesome God, who keeps his covenant of love with those who love him and keep his commandments, let your ear be attentive and your eyes open to hear the prayer your servant is praying before you day and night for your servants, the people of Israel. I confess the sins we

Israelites, including myself and my father's family, have committed against you. We have acted very wickedly toward you. We have not obeyed the commands, decrees and laws you gave your servant Moses.

Remember the instruction you gave your servant Moses, saying, 'If you are unfaithful, I will scatter you among the nations, but if you return to me and obey my commands, then even if your exiled people are at the farthest horizon, I will gather them from there and bring them to the place I have chosen as a dwelling for my Name.'

They are your servants and your people, whom you redeemed by your great strength and your mighty hand. Lord, let your ear be attentive to the prayer of this your servant and to the prayer of your servants who delight in revering your name. Give your servant success today by granting him favor in the presence of this man."

I was cupbearer to the king. (Nehemiah 1:4-11)

Notice the elements of this prayer and the fact that Nehemiah combined prayer with fasting, another *following skill*. In this prayer Nehemiah:

- Praised and extoled God's nature and character[11]
- Requested that God attend to his prayer
- Confessed his sins and the sins of his people Israel
- Called to remembrance God's Word and promises. (God does not need us to *remind* Him of what He has said. Instead, this is a common practice that demonstrates trust that God keeps His Word.)
- Revered God's name and implied commitment to obey and follow the Lord
- Asked specifically for success in speaking with the king

This is one of the lengthier prayers recorded in the Bible, yet one can read it in barely over one minute. Granted, the full extent of Nehemiah's prayer may have been longer, but God is not impressed with the length of our prayers. That's not what prayer is about.

Nehemiah prayed in desperation for his people, for himself, and for God to act on their behalf. We can tell from this prayer and what follows in context that God had already placed it on Nehemiah's heart to ask the king if he might go to Jerusalem and help rebuild the wall. In accord with God's will, Nehemiah prayed for the success only God could bring about.

Other prayers of Nehemiah recorded in Nehemiah are short, spontaneous prayers of a man of action. We read about one of those prayers in chapter 2:4. There, in the middle of a conversation with the king, Nehemiah shoots up a silent prayer to God for help, "Then I prayed to the God of heaven, and I answered the king."

I doubt whether Nehemiah said, "Ah, excuse me, Oh King Artaxerxes while I spend a few minutes in prayer." Instead, I think this was one of those silent prayers that we fire up to God in a split second when that's all we've got.

Men, think of Nehemiah in his context as a business man, entrepreneur, or site superintendent. He's a man of vision and action. He's in the thick of his work—work that he's good at—yet he pauses frequently "to pray to the God of heaven" for help.

A few years ago, I was reading in Colossians and read chapter 2:3, which says of Christ, "In whom are hidden all the treasures of wisdom and knowledge." On that day, when I read this verse I realized that we tend to compartmentalize Christ strictly into religious or spiritual categories. But as Creator of the universe, He possesses *all* wisdom and knowledge.

Whatever our area of expertise in our profession, we've got an expert Mentor and Consultant. We can go to God in prayer anytime about anything, anywhere. And God loves it when we consult Him!

At one point in my career I was the training manager of a large manufacturing facility. This particular plant (and industry) was fraught with challenges in the marketplace, including a labor dispute and an energy shortage. Frequently I was called upon to solve plant-wide hiring and training issues. I found tremendous relief and help from God as I turned to Him in prayer to help me with these challenges.

As I wrote the previous statement, I recognize that some may be of the opinion that God doesn't care about that stuff. On the contrary, He does care and He wants to hear from us about such issues or any issue in our lives for that matter.

When our kids were teenagers, my wife and I always invited them to share with us anything they were dealing with. Often, our teens would knock on our bedroom door at 10 pm. We'd invite them in and they'd throw themselves down on the foot of our bed and pour their hearts out. I'm sure you'd do the same with your kids. Our heavenly Father is even more attuned to our needs.

In the context of prayer Jesus commented, "If you, then, though you are evil, know how to give good gifts to your children, how much more will your Father in heaven give good gifts to those who ask him!" (Matthew 7:11) Our heavenly Father is infinitely more loving and caring than we will ever be. How could we expect less of Him than we are willing to provide for our children?

The Scriptures contain many more examples of prayers. One of the most bizarre prayers is the one Jonah prayed from the belly of a fish! Many of the Psalms are prayers and contain other elements of prayer that we haven't yet considered. Specifically, check out Psalm 6, 8, 9, 10, 12, 22, and 51.

There are some great prayers in Ezra 8:21-23 and 9:6. Also, look at Daniel 2:19-23 and 9:4. In the New Testament, we read Jesus' prayer for His disciples in John 17; some of the Apostles' prayers in Acts 1:24-25; 4:23-31; and Paul's prayer for churches in Ephesians 1:15-23; 3:14-21; and Colossians 1:9-14.

In those prayers we find praise, adoration, and thanksgiving toward God; requests on behalf of others; prayer for boldness; confession; and simply conversation and fellowship with the Lord. Basically, God wants us to talk to Him about anything and everything, anytime, and anywhere.

As you read through prayers that are recorded in Scripture, notice that those who pray often weave Scripture into their prayers. Acts 4:23-31 provides one example of this. Jesus also practiced this when He cried out on the cross, "My God, my God, why have you forsaken me." (Matthew 27:46) This is a quote (and a fulfillment of prophecy) from Psalm 22.

Picking up on this practice, I often weave Scripture into my prayers. Passages like Psalm 8:1, "Lord, our Lord, how majestic is your name in all the earth!" Or Psalm 73:25, "Whom have I in heaven but you? And earth has nothing I desire besides you." Or Psalm 90:2, "Before the mountains were born or you brought forth the whole world, from everlasting to everlasting you are God."

In times of distress or trouble I might draw from a passage like Hebrews 13:5, and pray, "Lord, thank You that You have promised never to leave me or forsake me." Sometimes when we're in anguish and our own words fail, a passage of Scripture comes to our rescue, "As the deer pants for streams of water, so my soul pants for you, my God." (Psalm 42:1)

Prayer is a learned skill

In the 2013 movie *Gravity*, Sandra Bullock's character, Dr. Ryan Stone laments in a life-threatening moment, "Nobody taught me how to pray." Communication is a *learned skill*. No infant is born talking. We all learned to talk and continue new and creative ways of expressing ourselves and understanding others for the rest of our lives.

The same is true in our communication with God. Jesus' disciples came to Him and asked, "Lord, teach us to pray." (Luke 11:1) Prayer is a learned skill—not a difficult one—but nonetheless learned. How can we hope to "hear" the Spirit of God unless we spend time conversing with Him? How else will we recognize His voice and be able to distinguish His from other "voices"?

When I first began following Jesus I found it more difficult to perceive His communication with me and distinguish His voice. The longer I've walked with Him, the easier this has become.

As we become familiar with the Word of God, it gets easier to hear and discern His voice. This makes sense since it is in His Word that we learn His character, His ways, and His dealings with mankind. Also, the example of other Christ followers and their coaching in our lives can be a tremendous help.

Instead of spending so much time and energy trying to figure out *how* the Holy Spirit speaks to us, we need to *trust* and *obey* Him when we *know* He is speaking to us.

A key truth I've discovered over the years is that if I come to God with a humble heart and a desire to do His will, I find it much easier to hear His voice. On the flip side, if I repeatedly disregard what the Spirit is saying to me, I will hear from Him less frequently and His voice becomes more difficult to perceive and distinguish from other voices.

Humble dependence is a primary characteristic of prayer to God. This is true both because we desperately need fellowship with Him and because we are totally dependent on Him for life itself. "For in him we live and move and have our being." (Acts 17:28) Our heavenly Father delights in our conversation with Him and wants us to come to Him for everything. Listen to Jesus' urgings to us on this matter:

> *Ask and it will be given to you; seek and you will find; knock and the door will be opened to you. For everyone who asks receives; he who seeks finds; and to him who knocks, the door will be opened.*
>
> *Which of you, if his son asks for bread, will give him a stone? Or if he asks for a fish, will give him a snake? If you, then, though you are evil, know how to give good gifts to your children, how much more will your Father in heaven give good gifts to those who ask him! (Matthew 7:7-11)*

Why is it then, that we ask for things sometimes and don't receive them—especially really good things—like someone's healing? It's precisely on this subject that prayer must be so relational and so personal.

Prayer does not attempt to convince God to do something He does not want to do. Rather, through prayer we seek to understand God's desire or plan in a situation and join with Him, asking Him to bring it about. "Your kingdom come, your will be done on earth as it is in heaven." (Matthew 6:10)

In the Garden of Gethsemane in anticipation of his arrest, humiliation and crucifixion, Jesus prayed in agony, "I want your will to be done, not mine." (Matthew 26:39 NLT) In prayer he set his will to do the will of the Father and in that will He endured the cross "for the joy set before him." (Hebrews 12:2) You and I must take the same attitude Jesus did with regard to the Father's will in prayer. Prayer is so much more than merely asking for things.

Two-and-a-half years ago, I got to know a couple in our church. The first time I met them, James had just been diagnosed with an inoperable brain tumor that would soon take his life. When James and his wife Heather received the news they prayed like they'd never prayed before. They had two grade-school age children at the time.

Obviously in a situation like this our go-to response is to pray for healing. The church elders and a host of other

Christ-followers from all over the country prayed for James' healing.

But as James and Heather prayed and drew closer to the Lord and each other through their prayers, they clearly heard the Lord tell them that He wanted to be glorified through James' death, rather than through his healing.

Because James and Heather listened to the Holy Spirit and trusted and obeyed Him, they purposed to live out the next few months together for the glory of God. And how they did! Everyone they came into contact with experienced encouragement, hope and love. No one left the same after visiting James and Heather.

When James passed away a few months later, his wife, two young children, and both sets of grandparents mourned profoundly. But even in their mourning they drank deeply from the well of God's mercy and compassion as they turned to Him in prayer. In times like those the Holy Spirit "intercedes for us through wordless groans." (Romans 8:26)

Prayer is a skill and discipline in which we'll never cease to grow and find new ways of expression and new opportunities in which to apply it. Just as we cannot learn to swim without getting in the water, we cannot learn to pray without immersing ourselves in it on all occasions.

Never stop praying. (1 Thessalonians 5:17 NLT)

The simplicity of prayer

On the previous pages, we established that prayer is a personal conversation with God. Understanding this definition of prayer also helps us eliminate other harmful prayer practices.

Early in my walk with Jesus, I thought it efficient to bring an agenda or list with me to prayer every day. So I kept a notebook with a list, which morphed into numerous lists. In fact, eventually, I had a separate list to pray through for each day of the week. I would come to prayer thinking I had to *get through my list* with God or I hadn't prayed.

Reflecting back on those days I'll make at least two observations. First, with that pattern for prayer *I rarely heard from God*, because I was doing all the talking. Second, because my prayers focused solely on working through a list, my prayers were lopsided. All I was doing was asking for stuff. Sure, I was praying for others, which is important. I was asking mostly for good stuff, but prayer is so much more than that.

I must also confess that my lists bored me to no end—not the people or items on the list—but the repetition of going through the lists. And my boredom often put me to sleep. My prayers seemed dry, lifeless, and powerless.

Another pattern I can remember from those early days is that my mind would wander. I'd be praying along and all of a sudden I was thinking about a hike, or a movie, or someone I'd met, or a totally unrelated event. And I remember thinking, "Where did that come from? Why am I thinking about that?" This tendency would frustrate me and caused me to feel guilty about losing my concentration with God. This sense of inadequacy undermined my confidence in coming to God in prayer.

During that time I also viewed prayer in a very compartmentalized fashion. I viewed prayer as a good work—*a Christian thing to do*, so I prayed every morning. But I was more focused on *my performance* in praying and less on the Lord. I would come to prayer relationally "detached" as I worked through my lists.

I trust by now that you've noticed a pattern in what I've described from my early attempts at praying. I was preoccupied with *myself* and *trying to impress God*. But God isn't interested in our trying to impress Him, He wants us to love Him and spend time with Him. Prayer is *communion with* and *conversation* with Him.

Today, prayer is very different for me. Prayer is not an end in itself like it used to be, but a means to enjoying God and conversing with Him often throughout the day. We often view prayer, Bible study, or one of the other following skills as "one more thing on my to-do list." Let me dispel that notion.

Think about tasks in your life that are so integrated into your life that you don't think twice about them. Who in their right mind would consider: brushing their teeth, showering, eating, going to bed at night, or kissing their wife and children as drudgery, "as just...one more thing they have to add to their to-do list!"

Nobody says, "I don't have time to brush my teeth anymore, so I'm going to eliminate that from my life." We integrate these tasks into our lives as foundational practices of good hygiene and healthy relationships. I encourage you to look at prayer in the same way. Integrate it into your life as a basic need of life instead of one more thing to add to the list.

At the risk of setting some kind of standard for prayer I'll share with you how I pray today. But you must meet with Jesus in a manner consistent with how He made you and in the season of life in which you find yourself. I also confess that I still consider myself a novice at prayer. I'm ever learning how to commune with my heavenly Father.

I still maintain a morning time of prayer (because I'm a morning person), but it looks very different than it used to. I'm usually the first one up in my household, so I get up and make a hot beverage and then sit on the couch and converse with the Lord. On a warm day, I'll go out onto the deck to pray. I come to Him each day eager to meet with Him and desirous of His company. I really look forward to this time each day.

In recent years, I find myself *listening* more than *talking*. I usually go over my day with the Lord and pray for those with whom I expect to meet. I ask for God's help, wisdom, and love as I deal with people and situations. I pray for other's welfare, healing, and God's provision in their lives.

When I'm praying, there are times in which I feel compelled to kneel humbly before God or stand and lift my hands to Him in praise. At other times I pray-walk or pray-hike in a place of solitude. I also frequently pray in the car.

I now realize that my wandering mind is sometimes due to the leading of His Holy Spirit. So rather than resist that tendency, I pray for that individual or situation that just came to mind. If my mind truly is just wandering, then I simply refocus on the Lord. I'm less concerned with my performance and more concerned with meeting with God.

As I pray, I worship Him, thank Him, praise Him and reflect on all He has done for my family and is currently doing in my life. Daily I confess my sins and I invite Him to change me. He often reveals to me where I need to guard myself in temptation so I can take preventative action.

When I pray for someone, I often use my imagination—a skill which Richard Foster helped me cultivate.[12] Our imagination—the creative faculty of our minds—must be transformed by Jesus just like the rest of us (see Romans 12:1-2). But without the imagination we cannot think creatively, problem-solve, or even read a book.

When we apply the imagination to prayer we don't do so in the sense that we pretend or fantasize. Rather, we ask God to help us envision what he wants to accomplish and then pray in faith accordingly. For instance, if I'm praying for a couple who is struggling in their marriage today, I might envision them walking on a beach, holding hands and totally in love with each other. I'll pray that their relationship is restored to that level of intimacy. That's how I use my imagination in prayer.

Read some of the prayers recorded in the Bible and notice how those praying enlisted the aid of their imaginations in framing their prayers. See Nehemiah 1:4-11; Psalms 130 and 139; Acts 4:23-30; Ephesians 1:15-23; 3:14-21.

A significant difference in my praying today is that my morning prayer serves as more of an opening conversation with God that will go on throughout the day. We can talk with Him anywhere, anytime, and about anything.

Praying on-the-spot

One of the most powerful applications of prayer that I have learned I received from my dad. Whenever someone asks for prayer, we usually say something like, "I'll be praying for you." Instead, say, "May I pray for you right now?" I've had more people tell me how powerful and meaningful this is. So don't underestimate its value.

I call this *praying on-the-spot* for people. Praying on-the-spot for others does three things that the standard response, "I'll be praying for you," does *not* accomplish. First, on-the-spot praying *takes action right now*. For many Christians, the phrase, "I'll be praying for you," has become nothing more than a polite cliché. We know good and well that our glib promise to pray for someone probably won't happen because we'll forget.

Praying on-the-spot for someone often takes them (pleasantly) by surprise. I remember one time a couple of us were listening to a woman tell us about the trials she was currently experiencing. I asked her if we could pray for her right now. In surprise she asked, "Can you do that?" (In other words, "Is that allowed?") I smiled and said, "Of course! Let's pray." She was visibly moved by and grateful for our prayer for her.

I've prayed on-the-spot for people countless times and many times for those who don't yet know the Lord. As of yet, I've never had anyone turn me down.

Second, praying on-the-spot openly demonstrates our love and care for an individual. Not only were we listening when they expressed their need for prayer, but we're praying for them *right now*. We're ushering them into the presence of God and pleading with Him on their behalf. This is tremendously encouraging to people and powerful. "The prayer of a righteous person is powerful and effective." (James 5:16)

The third thing that praying on-the-spot uniquely accomplishes is that it models for others a life of prayer. It's declaring, "We can pray anywhere, anytime, for anything." And it demonstrates how to pray. I learned how to pray on-the-spot unwittingly by simply watching my dad do it. Others have learned from me and now others will learn from you.

Practice

As you meet with the Lord for prayer each day this week, think about who you will meet during the day and pray for those individuals. Also, look for opportunities throughout your day to pray with people on-the-spot. You'll have to be attentive, because they may not specifically ask for prayer. They may express a need, trouble, or event in their lives that warrants prayer. Simply ask them, "May I pray for you right now?" And pray.

Discussion Questions

1. Why is it so important to recognize that prayer is a learned skill? How have you learned to pray?

2. In your walk with Christ so far, what means has He used to help you learn to pray? What has been most helpful for you?

3. Pick three of the following Psalms 6, 8, 9, 10, 12, 22, or 51, read those three Psalms and describe what David was praying for. How can you apply this to your prayers?

4. How does the Lord speak to you? How do you recognize His voice?

5. Discuss the comment, "Prayer is not convincing God to do something He doesn't want to do." Why do we often go into prayer thinking that convincing God is the focus?

6. Tell about a time when you trusted God for something major in your life. (Something that was significant for you.) What role did prayer play in that situation?

7. How has God recently answered prayer in your life?

8. This week look for new opportunities to pray, new things to pray for, and new ways to pray. Document your experience here.

9.   Pray with and for each other. We will go over the guidelines of praying with others in chapter 5, but for now simply follow these practices as you pray with each other:

- Pray *short*, phrase or sentence prayers (Don't hog the conversation!)
- Listen to the Holy Spirit and each other
- Piggyback on each other's prayers. Stay on a theme until it seems right to move on
- Keep your prayers vertical (God-ward)
- Embrace silence as an opportunity to listen to God, transition to another topic, or process what has been prayed
- Believe the best of each other

---

[11] God's *nature* refers to the attributes of God that are amoral: He is all-powerful, all-knowing, all-present. God's *character* speaks specifically of His moral qualities: He is holy, loving, just, righteous, gracious, merciful, etc.

[12] Richard Foster, *Celebration of Discipline*, (San Francisco: Harper, 1978, 1988, 1998), p. 41.

– Chapter 5 –

PRAYING CONVERSATIONALLY
WITH OTHERS

*Devote yourselves to prayer, being watchful and
thankful. Colossians 4:2*

When God's people pray together

Praying with other followers of Christ can be one of the
most exhilarating and meaningful experiences in our
relationship with the Lord and others. There is
something holy and powerful afoot when God's children
approach him with one voice seeking His glory!

I love it when Luke records of the newly formed church in Jerusalem, "They devoted themselves to the apostles' teaching and to fellowship, to the breaking of bread and to *prayer*. Everyone was filled with awe at the many wonders and signs performed by the apostles." (Acts 2:42-43)

On the other hand, praying with others may sometimes frustrate and demoralize us like little else can, leaving us feeling less than powerful and certainly less than holy.

I've already shared with you my pilgrimage through prayer and how I grappled early on to understand what prayer is and how to converse with God. My struggle with corporate prayer—praying with others—was even more intense.

I still remember a prayer meeting I was involved in many years ago. I was an elder in a church at the time. A number of us had come together to pray fervently for the church during a particularly crucial season. But a couple hours into the prayer meeting I became so frustrated and filled with confusion that I quietly, but stubbornly left. Something had gone really wrong!

As I drove home, I was in turmoil. I didn't know or understand why, but I felt angry, frustrated and confused. I felt *guilty* for leaving, yet a tremendous *relief* to be gone. I wrestled with the Lord about all these things all the way home and for some time afterward. I knew of no sin or conflict with others that could have triggered my response. Not until well over a year later did I begin to understand what had happened to me in that prayer meeting.

I know I'm not alone in the way I felt in that prayer meeting. I would venture to guess that many followers of Jesus sincerely struggle with their desires when the church calls a *prayer meeting*.

Even the term *prayer meeting* evokes visions of the saints moaning long-winded monologues in unearthly tones, employing vocabulary long since abandoned for everyday use!

In such prayer meetings we may feel grossly out of place and guilty for feeling that way. Is that really as good as it gets? Or have we unwittingly accepted a cheap counterfeit for something that God intended to be inviting, stimulating, and even *enjoyable*? The early church was "devoted...to prayer." (Acts 2:42) Where have we gone wrong?

Let me offer one chief reason for our dilemma by means of an analogy. Imagine that you are with a group of Christian friends. You're having pizza together and simply enjoying each other's company. As the evening progresses, you're all drawn to a topic about which you are passionate. But as you are about to launch into this conversation, one of your friends emphatically insists that the group impose the following *nine rules* to govern your discussion:

1. You must decide before-hand who will begin the conversation.
2. This discussion must flow around the circle, one person after another in order.
3. You may speak only once during this conversation.
4. You must speak for at least two minutes (the longer the better) when your turn comes around.
5. Think through what you will say before your turn comes.
6. When it's your turn to speak, try not to repeat a thought that has already been stated. Doing so would reveal your lack of creative thought.
7. If it comes to your turn and you do not wish to speak, simply sit there—say nothing and do nothing, just look down.
8. Deem silence as *uncomfortable* during this conversation. So if it's someone else's turn to speak and they don't immediately take their turn, the next person in the circle should resume the conversation quickly as if nothing happened.
9. The conversation is over when the last person in the circle has taken his/her turn.

Chances are that you and the others at your pizza party would laugh your friend's suggestion into oblivion! How ridiculous it would be to shackle our conversation with rules like this. It would be crazy! *And yet this is precisely what we often do when we pray together.*

In case those nine rules sounded familiar to you but you couldn't place them, think about how many of us learned to pray with others following rules like those. Oh, I doubt that anyone actually taught us these rules in the form of "Thou shalt." Rather, we simply adopted these behaviors through the example of others and they became norms.

Rules like these would be stifling, restrictive and deadly to healthy conversation with others. *Such rules are equally destructive in praying conversationally with others.*

Years after leaving the prayer meeting that I described above, I realized that my anger and frustration were largely due to the ridiculous protocol to which we had confined ourselves. We had tried to force corporate prayer into a *non-relational, non-conversational* process.

When I walked out on that prayer meeting, the man who was praying had been at it for 20 minutes without coming up for air. That's not praying with others, it's reciting a monologue. If he were a senator we'd call it *filibuster.*

Remember where we began in this book? We talked a lot about our relationship with our heavenly Father, with Jesus Christ and his Holy Spirit. We've also seen how we go astray when we stop thinking about our connection with the Lord as *relational*. But those crazy prayer rules above are anything but relational. They're stiff, stogy and impersonal. No wonder we run the other way when someone calls, "Prayer meeting!"

Principles of dynamic group prayer

So what does healthy, relational corporate prayer look and feel like? In conversational prayer with others, we primarily have to focus on relationships—both God-ward and man-ward. Relationships run well when we understand and operate within what is considered *gracious social protocol*.

So think about the process by which we conduct a lively, healthy, relational conversation and let's apply similar principles to praying together. By the way, these principles are not some secular, modern, psycho-babel! This is the way God created us. He created us relational beings. He is all about relationships: our relationship with Him and with others. After all, what is praying together but a *conversation* with the Lord and each other?

Principles for dynamic conversational prayer:[13]

- Pray *short*, phrase or sentence prayers (Don't hog the conversation!)
- Listen to the Holy Spirit and each other
- Piggyback on each other's prayers. Stay on a theme until it seems right to move on

- Keep your prayers vertical (God-ward)
- Embrace silence as an opportunity to listen to God, transition to another topic, or process what has been prayed
- Believe the best of each other

Let's look at each of these principles for conversational prayer more closely. *Pray short, phrase or sentence prayers.* Next time you find yourself in a lively, interesting conversation with others listen to the length of comments made by those involved in the conversation. Generally, comments are very short. In fact, if someone goes on for more than 30 seconds or a minute, the conversation has just degenerated to a monologue.

> *A man who prays much in private will make short prayers in public. D.L. Moody*

As you pray together, *listen to the Holy Spirit and to each other.* In group prayer there is a relational dynamic at work in which each of us wants to hear from the Lord and align our prayers and our lives with His desires and plan. And remember that God often speaks to us through others. Therefore our focus should be on *listening*—both to His Spirit and to others as they pray.

If all we are focused on is what we're going to say when it's our turn to pray, we can't listen to the prayers of others and we're not entering into group prayer. Also, without *listening* we cannot enter into the next principle.

Piggyback on each other's prayers. Stay on a theme until it seems right to move on. I cannot emphasize enough how important this principle is. Consider a normal conversation in which you make, what you believe is an important contribution to the conversation. What if the next person who speaks changes the subject totally, ignoring your comment? Wouldn't you feel unappreciated and wonder if anyone was even listening? Not following this simple principle is socially rude. But when we piggyback on each other's prayers, our prayers flow and we honor each other and the Lord. Our prayers become more effective as we demonstrate our care for each other and attend to the things that each person brings forward in prayer.

Keep your prayers vertical or God-ward. Many times I've sat in prayer meetings in which someone begins praying a very lengthy prayer that isn't a prayer at all. It's a lecture or sermon directed at the others in the room. I've even heard people use prayer as a device for shaming or heaping guilt on others present. We need to keep our motives pure and our focus on God. Pray to Him, not *at* others.

Embrace silence as an opportunity to listen to God, transition to another topic, or process what has been prayed. This principle brings up the point that we need to rehearse these principles with each other. We need to teach each other how to pray together and model effective group prayer with each other.

If everyone in our prayer group knows that a prolonged silence is okay, then people won't be recklessly scrambling to fill the void before they actually have something to say! In my experience, we find much freedom in this principle when we follow it.

Finally, *believe the best of each other*. Sometimes we may find ourselves praying with others whom we don't know well. They may pray something that seems weird or goofy, or they may use the wrong word in a context. That's okay, God knows their heart. Believe the best of each other. Listen to each other's prayers as our heavenly Father does.

The best way I've seen to implement these principles in a winsome and effective way is to rehearse them *every time* you come together to pray as a group. We might say something like, "In order to get the most out of our prayer time together, let's follow the principles of conversational prayer. Those are: ..." and then go over them very briefly.

During the five years we lived in Alaska, 250 to 350 Christ-followers rallied together to pray with each other every five to six weeks. We reviewed these principles of group prayer each time we came together to pray. Our church leadership reinforced that this prayer gathering was the "engine room" of the church. In five years I only missed a few of these dynamic prayer rallies due to travel.

I have seen these principles radically change the way followers of Christ pray together. Group prayer can become dynamic, engaging, relational, and very powerful.

Please don't mistake these principles for just another *clever way to pray*. These principles follow sound relational practices. We cannot ignore the way God designed us to relate with Him and others when we come together to pray. There are non-social behaviors that will hinder our relationships with each other and the Lord. Praying together should be a relational grace that bonds us with each other and our Lord.

In view of these principles of conversational prayer, I get excited about the prospect of "devoting ourselves to prayer." Consider how the conversational prayer must have gone in Acts 13:1-3 as the Lord revealed His will to the leadership of the church in Antioch. Or think about the fervor and tears—the deep relational connections as Paul and his entourage prayed with the elders from Ephesus before departing from them for the last time (Acts 20:17-38).

In the context of sound principles for conversational prayer, passages like Ephesians 6:18 become a rallying cry to action for the church. "And pray in the Spirit on all occasions with all kinds of prayers and requests. With this in mind, be alert and always keep on praying for all the saints." (That exhortation is written to the church corporately—as the pronouns are all *plural*.)

We find similar calls to group prayer in Colossians 4:2, "Devote yourselves to prayer," and in 1 Thessalonians 5:17, "Pray continually." When we pray together, we stand together in the presence of Almighty God and lift our voices to Him in praise, adoration, thanksgiving and with our requests. God loves it when his children converse with Him.

Let us not spoil what is good and holy and enjoyable by placing relationally destructive or confining practices on our group prayer.

A tip for a great marriage—pray with your wife!

Men, if you are married, one of the greatest things you can do to love and honor your wife and please the Lord is to pray with her daily. When a man (or a couple) comes to me for marriage coaching or counseling, one of the first things I ask the husband is whether he prays daily *with* his wife. As one brother recently put it, "We men would readily take a bullet for our wives, but rarely take a knee."[14]

If a man and wife are struggling in their marriage I can almost guarantee they're not praying together. On the flip side of that when a man and woman in a troubled marriage begin praying together, they not only draw closer to God but to each other as well.

Why is prayer so powerful in a marriage? I believe that God designed the husband to be the spiritual leader of the family. When he steps up to his responsibility and begins leading his wife and family into the presence of God, their lives are transformed. Remember, as we draw near to God, we cannot remain unchanged.

Peter was one of the twelve apostles who was married. In 1 Peter 3:7 he challenges us:

> *Husbands, in the same way be considerate as you live with your wives, and treat them with respect as the weaker partner and as heirs with you of the gracious gift of life, so that nothing will hinder your prayers.*

According this passage, there's a direct correlation between prayer and how we treat our wives.

Clearly, when we tenderly lead our wives into the presence of God as we pray out loud with them, we show them consideration and respect. We dare not approach God with bitterness in our hearts toward them. I pity the man who abuses his wife in any way and then dares approach God as though everything were fine between him and his Lord! God will judge that man most severely.

From 1 Peter 3:7, the reason that a man's maltreatment of his wife will hinder his prayers is because our relationship with our wife is intimately tied to our relationship with God. If we are at odds with our wife, we are at odds with God.

The principle Jesus gave in Matthew 5:23-24 applies here:

> Therefore, if you are offering your gift at the altar and there remember that your brother or sister has something against you, leave your gift there in front of the altar. First go and be reconciled to them; then come and offer your gift.

Men, we need to step up to our God-given responsibility and pray with our wives.

Like Peter pointed out in the above passage, our wives are generally weaker than we are physically. But isn't it strange how *weak* many men are when it comes to praying with their wives? So many men I've talked to are scared to death to pray with their wives. Let me suggest a couple of reasons for this.

The most obvious reason to me is that men typically find it more difficult to pray out loud with anyone. Men tend to be less verbally expressive and prayer calls on us to draw from our innermost being. Men aren't used to doing that, but we've got to learn.

Take lessons from King David. He was a mighty warrior and a king and yet he wrote and spoke things from deep within his soul. Read five Psalms a day for a month and let God's Word make you the man He wants you to become.

I pray with my wife Linda each morning and before we go to bed at night and sometimes in between. They're usually short prayers, but sometimes we have more to pray about and take advantage of a longer session of prayer. I often pray with her on-the-spot too, when she voices a worry or concern.

Be courageous and ask your wife if you could pray with her each day. Choose a time or times that allow you to make it a habit. Your prayers need not be long.

Hold her hand, put your arm around her, or embrace her. Simply thank God for her, ask Him to be with her, take care of her and prosper her throughout the day.

Pray something specific about her day asking God to especially help her in a meeting, or taking a child to the doctor, or whatever she's doing that day. If she would like to pray too, then give her that opportunity. If she chooses not to, that's okay.

Sharing your lives before the Lord like this will transform you!

Another reason some men may find it difficult to pray with their wives is if they've been abusing or mistreating them. If this is your situation, you know that if you ask your wife to pray with you right now you'll only be adding hypocrisy to your list of sins. Your only recourse is to ask both your wife and the Lord for forgiveness. Tell her you want to change.

You may need to work with a pastor or counselor if things are really going roughly. Men are dumb if they think they can abuse their wives for twenty years and expect them to forgive them in twenty minutes. Let your wife see and experience a genuinely transformed man. Give her room and reason to forgive.

Let me leave you with one more great reason to pray with your wife. For over 39 years, Linda and I have been praying together each day. One of the things we pray about is our own needs and those of others. As I shared earlier in this book, we are currently in a season of life in which we are trusting God day by day to meet our needs.

It's been three years since Linda has been able to visit her aging mother in South Carolina who is beginning to fail. We knew we needed to go see her, but it's literally across the country and we didn't have the funds to get there. So we began praying that the Lord would provide the funds for two round-trip tickets to Greenville, SC from Spokane, WA.

Meanwhile, totally unrelated to this, a friend of ours spontaneously urged us to go to a website to see if we had any *unclaimed property*. At first I dismissed the idea as some kind of scam, but then I learned of its legitimacy. We've lived in several states, so we checked them all. To our amazement, we had an insurance refund due us in Alaska for $504. (How we ever missed that is a mystery!) So we applied for our refund and within two weeks the check arrived!

When the $504 check arrived, I told my wife, "Honey, the Lord is providing our needs for a ticket to go see your mom." So Linda began checking on ticket prices. Because we were making flight arrangements far enough in advance we were able to get two round trip tickets for a total of $687.54. With the $504, we still needed $183.54 to make up the difference, so we prayed for that. We had told no one about this need.

The very next day, a friend of ours slipped an envelope in my hand and said that a mutual friend who wished to remain anonymous asked him to give it to us. Inside the envelope were two crisp one-hundred-dollar bills! We tithed the gift ($20) which left us $180 and we made up the difference of $3.54. Isn't God good!

Sharing an experience of God's provision like that with my wife is priceless. We both grow in our faith in Him and we learn to trust each other as well. Experiencing answers to prayer and God's provision like that continues to invest in our relationship with each other and with the Lord. Men, I urge you, pray with your wife!

Let me share one more example of how Linda and I pray together. In April 2012, my wife and I began sensing that the Lord wanted me to change careers. Both of us had begun feeling *complacent*—too comfortable—in our situation. I was 60 years old at the time and it would have been easy to hunker down in my job for a few more years. Many would argue that would've been the sensible thing to do.

I have discovered over the years, however, that we sometimes dictate to God what we will or won't do based on our *perception* of what is sensible. But down through history, God often asked people to do things that by the world's standards are outlandish!

For instance, God asked Abraham to leave his home country and kin and to start traveling west. God didn't even tell him where he was going. God basically said, "I'll let you know when you get there." God told Joshua to conquer Jericho by marching around its walls. "Really, You want me to do what?" Jesus told His disciples to feed a multitude with five loaves and two fish. And later He commanded them to go into all the world and preach the gospel. Instead of arguing with Him about how that's supposed to work, they just did it!

So, when God began speaking to my wife and me about changing careers, we prayed daily and in a focused manner to further discern His leading. God's leading in the lives of individuals is often very personal. What He asks of me, He may not ask of you.

In our case, Linda and I continued to pray through the summer. By the end of August, the Holy Spirit had impressed on us that He wanted me to resign my position as pastor of our church. In all our 39 years of marriage, Linda and I have understood from Scripture that we are one. So in issues like this, we must function as one. If God is really leading us, He will lead *both* of us—not just me, or only Linda.

With our decision reached, I met with our elders and explained what was happening. I agreed to stay on through October to help launch the fall programming.

When I resigned, we did not know what I was supposed to go to next. We only knew that God had led us to resign. He often leads us in this way, asking us to obey Him one step at a time and trust Him for the future.

Around the time I resigned, I also happened to reestablish contact with an old friend. We hadn't communicated with each other for many years. My friend's background and wiring are similar to mine. My friend, Tim, began sharing with me that he has been a life coach for the past seven years and absolutely loves it. The more he talked about coaching, the more it began to resonate with me.

At Tim's suggestion, I checked out a Christian life coach institute and tapped into other sources of information on life coaching. The more I researched coaching, the more I sensed the Holy Spirit leading me in this direction. I included Linda in this whole discussion and she heartily agreed.

We had a very limited amount of savings to live on until I could build up my business as a leadership coach (the direction I landed on). As you can imagine, the circumstances of these last fifteen months have driven us to prayer in a huge way.

We've prayed that God would: help me do well in my training and develop me into an accomplished coach; lead me to clients; grant me creativity, wisdom, and favor in my writing and speaking; and provide for our financial needs.

I'll be honest that this time has not all been easy for either of us. Occasionally, we've questioned: "Did we really hear God's voice in this decision?" "How are we going to make it financially?" "What if we run out of savings?" "Where are clients going to come from?" "Will my books sell?" And we've struggled over a host of other questions.

But the Lord has been so faithful. He said, "Never will I leave you; never will I forsake you." (Hebrews 13:5)

God has provided so creatively this past year, giving us everything we need. It occurred to me after I left my job to start a business that if we truly believe that God is our Provider and that everything comes from Him, then nothing has changed in our situation from that standpoint. God is now and always has been our Provider.

In addition to the financial side of things, I *love* coaching. I've narrowed my focus to leadership coaching, which has been a passion of mine for many years. Launching this business has also given me more time to write. I'm on track to publish five new books this year including this one. This is all to the Lord's credit. He asked us to trust Him in this venture and as we trust Him, He remains faithful.

This whole enterprise has been bathed in prayer. Linda and I pray every day both individually and together that God will lead us and meet our needs. I also experience the joy of entering into the lives of my clients and praying with and for them. By God's grace I have the pleasure of helping them meet their goals, increase their capacity for leadership, and improve on a wide variety of leadership skills.

Linda and I pray daily thanking God for what He is doing in our lives and the lives of those we serve. We pray simply praising Him and worshiping Him for His great goodness and love.

In telling you about all of this I hope to underscore that prayer is an every-day, practical, and dynamic *following skill*. Prayer defines a life of faith—a life living *on alert!*

Living by faith means living a life in constant prayer. Men, this dependent, abiding trust in the Lord is exactly where He wants us to live. "And without faith it is impossible to please him, for whoever would draw near to God must believe that he exists and that he rewards those who seek him." (Hebrews 11:6 ESV)

Conclusion

In this short book we've focused on the need to be *on the alert* and that prayer is one of the primary ways we maintain our vigilance. We've also emphasized Jesus' challenge to us to persevere in prayer. I'd like to bring this book to an end with a remarkable answer to prayer recorded in Luke 1.

Luke 1:5-25 tells the account of the birth of John the Baptist—the forerunner of the Messiah. Luke introduces us to Zechariah and his wife Elizabeth. "And they were both righteous before God, walking blamelessly in all the commandments and statutes of the Lord. But they had no child, because Elizabeth was barren, and both were advanced in years." (Luke 1:6-7 ESV)

In that day, the ability to have children was everything, but they had remained childless—first because Elizabeth was barren and now because they were both too old. Elizabeth had suffered disgrace among her people all these years because she had remained childless (Luke 1:25).

The angel Gabriel appeared to Zechariah while he was fulfilling his priestly duties in the temple. Gabriel announced to Zechariah, "Do not be afraid, Zechariah; *your prayer has been heard*. Your wife Elizabeth will bear you a son, and you are to call him John." (Luke 1:13) Stop for a moment and meditate on that. Let the significance of what Gabriel said to Zechariah sink in. *"Your prayer has been heard!"*

Zechariah did not respond immediately in faith and thanksgiving, but rather in skepticism and disbelief. "And Zechariah said to the angel, 'How shall I know this? For I am an old man, and my wife is advanced in years.'" (Luke 1:18 ESV)

Here's the point—Gabriel, who stands in the presence of God, declared that the birth of John the Baptist was in direct answer to Zechariah's prayers. Wow! Based on

Zechariah's response, we know that this prayer had to be an old prayer—a stale prayer. Zechariah would not have responded the way he did if he and Elizabeth were still in the habit of begging God daily for a child. No doubt Zechariah and Elizabeth had prayed for perhaps 30 years or more for a child. But when none came and they became old, they stopped praying.

And yet, here's Gabriel announcing, "Your prayer has been heard." Not only is this a very specific and loving response to their hearts' cry, but consider the significance that their answer to prayer was to be John the Baptist. Gabriel said, "He will be a joy and delight to you, and many will rejoice because of his birth, for he will be great in the sight of the Lord. He will be filled with the Holy Spirit even before he is born. He will bring back many of the people of Israel to the Lord their God." (Luke 1:14-16)

"When the fullness of time had come, God sent forth his Son." (Galatians 4:4 ESV) And in this fullness of time God answered Zechariah and Elizabeth's prayers for a child. The sovereign plan of God was at work and their prayers played a significant role in these world-changing events. Again, let that sink in.

Yet, there is one more amazing element to this delayed answer to prayer. God in His mercy, allowed Zechariah and Elizabeth to have John in their old age. By the time John was in his early 30s, he had ushered in Jesus, the

Messiah, and then he was beheaded by Herod. What a mercy it was that John's parents would have already passed away and would not have had to witness their beloved son's execution.

I stand in awe at the way God sovereignly and lovingly orchestrated these events in answer to an old, stale prayer. The answer to Zechariah and Elizabeth's prayer motivates me to, "Be alert and always keep on praying." (Ephesians 6:18)

As I bring this book to a close, we've seen that our Lord Jesus Christ has put us *on alert*. One of the primary ways we maintain our vigilance is through prayer. Through prayer we maintain constant contact with our Lord ready to perform His bidding at a moment's notice. Prayer keeps us in His presence attuned to His holiness and to the character changes He wants to bring about in us.

Being on alert in prayer helps us eliminate distractions and stay focused on Him and on what He deems important. Watchful in prayer, we look forward to Christ's return and to the joy of knowing that He will find us expectant and ready for Him. So pray and do not lose heart!

Practice

I want to leave you with two assignments from this last chapter. First, look for an opportunity to implement the principles of group prayer that I shared in this chapter.

You might introduce them to your small group, Men's ministry, or in a prayer meeting. Look for an opportunity to put these principles into practice within the next week. You can simply tell people that you have an assignment and ask if they would humor you. Then simply introduce the principles and pray together.

Second, if you're not already doing so, speak with your wife (if you're married) and ask her if the two of you could begin praying together every day. Start out very short—even if it means praying at the door as one or the other of you leaves for work. Establish this as a habit, a daily family tradition.

Discussion Questions

1. What was your biggest takeaway from this chapter?

2. What has been your experience with group prayer in the past? Have prayer meetings been something you run to or from?

3. Look back at the Principles for dynamic conversational prayer. Which one of these will most greatly impact group prayer for you? Why?

4. What is the significance of group conversational prayer? Why do you think the Scriptures emphasize it so strongly? (See Acts 2:42-43; Ephesians 6:18; Colossians 4:2.)

5. Why is praying with our wives so beneficial? What has your experience been in this regard?

6. In what ways has God answered prayer for you and your wife (if married)?

7. Rehearse with each other again how prayer enables us to *be on the alert*.

8. Pray with and for each other. We will go over the guidelines of praying with others in chapter 5, but for now simply follow these practices as you pray with each other:

- Pray *short*, phrase or sentence prayers (Don't hog the conversation!)
- Listen to the Holy Spirit and each other
- Piggyback on each other's prayers. Stay on a theme until it seems right to move on
- Keep your prayers vertical (God-ward)
- Embrace silence as an opportunity to listen to God, transition to another topic, or process what has been prayed
- Believe the best of each other

---

[13] I am deeply indebted to the leadership at ChangePoint who modeled these principles of conversational prayer.

[14] Bruce Snell at a gathering of pastors in Spokane, WA, Sept. 2013.

APPENDIX: ADDITIONAL RESOURCES

Calhoun, Adele Ahlberg. *Spiritual Disciplines Handbook*. Downers Grove, IL: Intervarsity Press, 2005.

Foster, Richard. *Celebration of Discipline*. New York: HarperCollins Publishers, 1998.

Smith, James Bryan. *The Good and Beautiful God*. Downers Grove, IL: Intervarsity Press, 2009,

Whitney, Donald S. *Spiritual Disciplines for the Christian Life*. Colorado Springs, CO: NavPress, 1991.

Willard, Dallas. *The Spirit of the Disciplines*. New York: HarperCollins Publishers, 1988.

OTHER BOOKS BY ROB FISCHER

Fully Equipped – *God's Word, One of the Essentials for Survival (This book is part of the Summit Leadership Series for Men.)*

Comrades in Arms – *The Power of Pursuing Christ in the Company of Other Men*

Rogue Principles *that Grow Church Community* – A small group curriculum and companion book to the movie *Rogue Saints*

Enthralled with God, 2nd Edition with Discussion Questions

Strategies for Discipleship – A Small Group Curriculum that Targets the Skills for Discipling Others

Becoming Tarzan – A humorous collection of childhood stories that appeal to the whole family

13 Jars – The true stories of women who found redemption, forgiveness and peace through Jesus Christ following their abortions

Be sure to look for future books by Rob in the *Summit – Leadership Series for Men!*

ABOUT THE AUTHOR

Rob has enjoyed a truly varied background! He served as a German linguist/cryptologist with the Army Security Agency during the Cold War in Berlin. He pastored two small churches, helped plant two churches in Austria as a missionary, and served on the staffs of two large churches in the US.

Rob also worked for Burlington Northern Railroad and Kaiser Aluminum providing leadership development training and managing the training function. Since 2012 Rob has owned his own coaching business: Fischer Leadership Coaching.

Rob has also been writing professionally for over 35 years. He has published 10 books, edited numerous other books, ghostwrites, blogs, and has published hundreds of articles on a wide array of topics.

Rob graduated from Moody Northwest; Northwestern College, MN (BA); Luther Rice Seminary, GA (MA); Amberton University, TX (MS); and is a Certified Professional Life Coach (Professional Christian Coaching Institute.)

Rob has been married to Linda for nearly 40 years and is blessed with three married children and eight grandchildren.

Rob enjoys hiking, bicycling, snowshoeing, cross-country skiing, reading and woodworking. He lives in Spokane Valley, WA.

Above all, Rob is a follower of Jesus Christ! He lives for Christ and seeks to glorify Him in all he does. Rob has a passion for discipling other followers of Christ and for the unborn. One of his deepest desires is to see the end of abortion in the US in his lifetime.

To contact Rob about his books or for coaching visit him online at: www.RobFischerAuthor.com.

Made in the USA
San Bernardino, CA
13 March 2014